# HOW TO GROW ROSES:
## *The Amateur's Guide*

# How to Grow Roses:

## The Amateur's Guide

BY VEVA PENICK WRIGHT

WITH ILLUSTRATIONS BY

GRAMBS MILLER

COPYRIGHT© 1967, 1972 BARRE PUBLISHERS

LIBRARY OF CONGRESS CATALOG CARD NUMBER 72-83361

INTERNATIONAL STANDARD BOOK NUMBER 8271-7240-0

BARRE PUBLISHERS BARRE, MASSACHUSETTS

DESIGN: SHIRLEY ERRICKSON

PRINTING: NIMROD PRESS

NOTE: This book was originally published under the title
*So You Want To Grow Roses.*

# Contents

9 ᘐ᠌ *Author's Foreword*

11 ᘐ᠌ *A Short History of the Rose*

16 ᘐ᠌ *Roses to Tempt You*

WHERE AND HOW TO BUY ROSES

ORDER ROSES FOR FALL OR SPRING PLANTING

DIG THEM UP!

POTTED OR PACKAGED ROSE PLANTS

THE AMERICAN ROSE SOCIETY

THE ROYAL NATIONAL ROSE SOCIETY

MODERN GARDEN ROSES

*Old, Rare, and Historic Roses*

GALLICA ROSES

DAMASK ROSES

CHINA ROSES (TEA)

SOME INTERESTING SPECIES NATIVE TO VARIOUS COUNTRIES

36 ᘐ᠌ *Choose the Planting Area with Care*

ROSES HAVE CERTAIN LIKES AND DISLIKES

MAKE A PLAN BEFORE YOU ORDER YOUR ROSES

39 ᘐ᠌ *The Good Earth*

SOIL

HUMUS (ORGANIC MATTER)

TEST YOUR SOIL

PH

DRAINAGE

PREPARE THE ROSE BED PROPERLY

50 *The Roses Arrive*

ROSES ARRIVE FOR SPRING PLANTING
ROSES ARRIVE FOR FALL PLANTING
GETTING READY TO PLANT
PLANTING DIRECTIONS
PROTECT ROSES PLANTED IN SPRING
PROTECT ROSES PLANTED IN FALL
PLANTING POTTED OR PACKAGED ROSES
TRANSPLANTING ROSES

61 *Mulches*

MULCHES (ORGANIC)
HOW TO APPLY THE MULCH
WHEN TO APPLY THE MULCH

66 *Watering*

HOW TO WATER THE ROSE BEDS
SPECIAL WATERING CARE FOR SOILS OF DIFFERENT TEXTURES
WATERING EQUIPMENT

71 *The Roses' Diet*
*Balance the Diet*

INORGANIC FERTILIZERS (CHEMICALS - MINERALS)
THE MINOR OR TRACE ELEMENTS ARE:
ORGANIC FERTILIZERS (NATURE'S FOOD)
*Feeding Established Roses*
WHEN, WHAT AND HOW TO FEED
COMPLETE ROSE FOODS ARE AVAILABLE IN THREE FORMS:
THE FIRST MEAL IN SPRING SHOULD BE ORGANIC
THE SECOND MEAL IN SPRING
THE THIRD MEAL
*Feeding Newly Planted Roses*

83 *Pruning*

SPRING PRUNING — WHEN AND HOW
SUMMER PRUNING
FALL PRUNING

94 *The Rose and Its Problems*
*Diseases and Insect Pests*

*A Guide to Common Diseases of Roses*
*Fungus Diseases of Roses*
BLACKSPOT — DIPLOCARPON ROSAE
MILDEW — (SPHAEROLTECA PANNOSO ROSEA)
RUST — (PRAYMIDIUM MUCRONATUM)
CANKER — "WOUND" FUNGI
DIEBACK
*Crown and Root Problems*
CROWN GALL — ROUNDED TUMOR OR WOUND DISEASE
CROWN CANKER
*Hidden Hunger*
CHLOROSIS
SOME COMMON CAUSES OF CHLOROSIS:
MORE LEAF PROBLEMS — PHOSPHORUS AND POTASH
        DEFICIENCIES
VIRUS INFECTION
PURPLE SPOTTING
*Insect Pests*
*Spraying or Dusting is Serious Business*
SPRAYING VS. DUSTING
SYSTEMIC INSECTICIDES — (NOT FUNGICIDES)
DORMANT SPRAYS — (FUNGICIDES)
EQUIPMENT NEEDED
*Chemical Controls*
132 &ᴗ *Winter Protection*
WINTERIZE YOUR PLANTS
138 &ᴗ *It's Spring Again*
THERE'S WORK TO DO
SPRING CHORES
142 &ᴗ *Glossary*
145 &ᴗ *Visit Public Rose Gardens and Nurseries*
SOME ROSE GARDENS IN THE UNITED STATES
FAMOUS ROSE GARDENS OF EUROPE
148 &ᴗ *Bibliography*
151 &ᴗ *Accredited Rose Growers of the United States and Canada*
153 &ᴗ *Index*

# FOREWORD

This book is not a treatise on the rose. It has been written for the pleasure of the would-be rosarian, and is factual, practical, informative. It will, I hope, help you enjoy tending your roses and give you some simple advice — so hard to come by!

Roses are not difficult to grow when the basic do's and don'ts are understood. The rules are easy to learn and simple to apply; and after the first year, even the rosarians' scientific terms become ABC's.

Roses of today are more productive than roses of "yesteryear," for science and experience, over hundreds of years, have helped rosarians to develop better methods of hybridizing and cultivation. These new varieties, of which there are several thousands, produce larger blooms and have more brilliant colors than those of their ancestors.

The rose, one of the most decorative and adaptable of all flowers, may be used in garden schemes as hedges, borders, or ornamentals; certain varieties blend with flowering shrubs, evergreens, and perennials. The climbing and pillar types give color to fences and trellises and transform unsightly buildings into lovely walls of color in spring. The rambler rose, trailing over banks along the roadsides in early summer, is nature's way of covering scars. Many of these wild roses are colorful in the fall when the rose hips cover the bush with red-brown fruit.

Roses are hardy plants. They tolerate hurricanes that strip away their leaves, ice storms that blacken their canes, and humidity that encourages fungus spores of mildew to tarnish their summer beauty; but after their winter's rest, come spring, pink leaf buds proclaim the rose's readiness to forgive the elements and produce again.

# A Short History of the Rose

The genealogy of the rose is difficult to trace. It is in fact so complicated we leave the subject to the scientifically inclined rosarian, and trace briefly the rose's impact on man throughout the history of civilization.

The wild rose, pre-historic ancestor of our modern rose, was a rambling briar-type plant with small pink or white flowers, often fragrant. Different species of wild roses can be found in every corner of the Northern Hemisphere from Arctic regions to mountains and deserts, but no rose has yet been discovered indigenous to the Southern Hemisphere.

The rose is possibly the oldest cultivated flower and is believed to ante-date man! This theory has recently been substantiated by geologists' discovery in Colorado and Oregon of fossilized roses believed to be thirty-five to seventy million years old.

When the rose is brought into the garden, it not only brings flowers and fragrance, but opens avenues of interest rarely attributed to any flower. While tracing its history, the inquirer is taken into literature, poetry, music, medicine, even cookery. Throughout the ages historians have recorded its genealogy and uses, poets have extolled its beauty, painters, architects, and sculptors have used its form to embellish cathedrals, buildings, and tombs. In 800 B.C. Homer wrote in the Odyssey of the "rosy-fingered dawn" and in 600 B.C. Sappho, the poetess, named the rose Queen of Flowers.

The perfume of roses drifted through ancient gardens of Persian and Chinese emperors, and Babylonian manuscripts describe the Hanging Gardens of Babylon and tell of Nebuchadnezzar having roses planted in the garden to please his favorite wife, Amytis.

The wild rose was imported to the Nile Valley of Egypt probably from Persia. The Egyptians, delighted with this fragrant flower, cultivated the *species rosa* and used it in many ways. They extracted oil and attar from the rose, used the perfume lavishly in their homes, and kept their bodies saturated with its various fragrances. History tells us that Nefertiti's beautiful young body was daily rubbed with oil and attars.

Archeologists have found, upon opening some Egyptian tombs, well-preserved garlands of roses laid hundreds of years before on the golden coffins of the Pharaohs.

During the reign of the Ptolemies, roses became a fad, and we read that Cleopatra, wishing to please Anthony, had the palace floor strewn twenty inches deep with roses and then had them covered with a fine net so he could walk on them. Later, the story goes, Anthony requested Cleopatra to have his bier covered with roses and to have roses planted around his tomb.

The lavish use of roses in Egypt created so great a market for blooms that the Egyptians had to develop enormous rose nurseries to supply their needs. They shipped roses to Rome, but history does not explain how the blossoms were kept fresh during their long voyage.

The Greeks were already skilled in the art of gardening when the wild rose was first brought to the Greek Isles. They, too, cultivated the rose and created the first market for cut flowers.

Pliny, the Roman naturalist, in his *Natural History* has identified, recorded, and listed form, color, and growing habits of these ancient varieties, thereby giving invaluable information to present-day hybridizers.

The first known beauty cream was developed by the famous Greek physician, Galen. His basic formula, using white wax, oil of roses, rose water, and rose vinegar, is still used for modern cold creams.

When the Romans became interested in roses to decorate their palaces for banquets and festivals, they bought rose plants and flowers from

Greece and Egypt. Later to satisfy the great demand for roses, the Romans developed their own vast nurseries, and eventually built fabulous greenhouses heated by clay pipes filled with hot water to induce the rose to bloom out of season.

Obsessed by the rose, the Romans wore the flowers, slept on them, ate the petals, and had "wine of roses" for their banquets. Nero is said to have filled his fountains with rose-water and paid four million sesterces for blossoms to decorate the palace for one feast.

In ancient history we find Seneca's protest against the debauchery of these Roman feasts and festivals where "slaves as well as statues" were bedecked with garlands of roses, and where petals "showered like rain," sometimes suffocating guests.

Romans used all parts of the rose for medicinal purposes; the powdered and liquid forms were concocted to cure such ailments as "loose teeth, hangover, watering eyes, and to wash the molligrubs out of the brain."

After the fall of the Roman Empire, the glorious era of the rose seemed to end, for having been used in pagan ceremonies and festivals, it was rejected by the Christians and played no part in early Christian civilization. Fortunately, many important varieties were preserved by being secretly cultivated during those troubled years in private gardens, convents, and monasteries. It is believed that the first prayer beads were made from roses and rose hips, hence the name, Rosary.

When the Crusaders returned to England and France from war in foreign lands, they brought seeds of new species of roses and beautiful designs depicting the rose. These designs were immediately accepted by Christian architects for ecclesiastical use and developed into designs that are now famous as rose windows.

In medieval times, knights wore roses as emblems of their ladies' love, and ladies of the court embroidered dresses and religious vestments with rose designs.

In addition to being employed for romantic and decorative purposes, roses were grown extensively for their medicinal value. Apothecaries processed every part of the rose into dried or liquid forms for use as tonics and astringents besides concocting remedies for almost every ailment.

During the Napoleonic Wars, surgeons and physicians were dispatched by Napoleon to the town of Provins near Paris to obtain special medicines made from dried rose petals and hips of the Provins rose (often called the Apothecarys' rose) that he believed to be necessary for his soldiers' health. (Could this curative value have been Vitamin C? During World War II the English and Scots found the wild rose hips to be four hundred times richer in Vitamin C than oranges.) For many years the roots and sap of the wild rose, so common to the woodlands of France and England, were supposed to cure rabies if processed in a particular way. This wild pink rose is still known as the Dog Rose, or *Rosa canina*.

To show the longevity and determination of the *species Rosa*, there is a climbing rose growing at the Abbey of Hildesheim in Germany, supposedly planted by Charlemagne, that is said to be a thousand years old! This rose, thirty feet high, covers forty feet of the abbey wall. During World War II air raids damaged the abbey, but the rose, undisturbed lives on.

The Isle of Rhodes claimed its name from the rose (*rhodon*) in 408 B.C. To commemorate the naming of the Isle the rose motif was used to imprint their coins. The obverse side of the coin was imprinted with the head of Helios, the sun god, and the rose used on the reverse side of all coins until the Isle of Rhodes was absorbed into the Roman Empire in 43 B.C.

The role the rose has played in the economy of nations is in itself a fascinating subject. Not only has there been a tremendous market created for rose plants and flowers but many nations throughout the centuries have used the rose motif to imprint their coins.

The rose was made the floral emblem of England in 1481. England has used the rose motif to embellish her coins for hundreds of years, and still uses it. It is interesting to note that a coin, the Gold Crown of the Double Rose, was struck in 1526 and carried the motto, "Henry VIII, the dazzling rose without thorns." The first coin sent to the American colonists by the British in 1722 had the rose depicted on it. This coin, known as the "Rosa Americana," was lovely to look at, but had such a small quantity of silver in it that it proved unpopular with the American colonists, and they refused to use it. Many of these coins can be seen in museums or in private coin collections.

Our modern garden rose dates from the early eighteenth century, when French gardeners and rosarians were stimulating interest in rose culture. But it was Josephine, Empress of France, who gave the greatest impetus to the development of the rose when, soon after 1800, she summoned the leading rose authorities to design for her the famous rose gardens at Malmaison and appointed André DuPont to supervise her roses. It is interesting to note here that up until this period roses had been hybridized by the processes of nature and that André DuPont was the first to attempt artificial hybridizing with the many rose species available at Malmaison. It is recorded that 256 varieties of roses were collected for Josephine's gardens. By 1829 hybridizers had developed and named more than 2,000 varieties.

Josephine not only encouraged the development of the rose, she commissioned artists, sculptors, and craftsmen of all kinds to depict the beauty of her favorite flower. Of these, the painter Pierre Joseph Redouté became the most famous when in 1817-1824 he compiled his exquisite paintings into three volumes called *Les Roses*. These paintings are still considered to be among the finest depicting the rose.

In cookery, rose petals have been used for hundreds of years as "sweet-meats." In a cookbook called *A Queen's Delight*, published in 1695, recipes are given for sugaring rose petals. These rose confections are still made in France and are a favorite decoration for cakes and candies.

In our own country we have a lovely white briar rose brought us by Spanish explorers that sprawls over countryside and mountains, known as the Cherokee Rose. An old Indian legend tells that Cherokee braves gathered these wild roses for their brides to braid in their hair, believing these lovely flowers insured eternal love.

Rose products are still being used in this modern age. The greatest sources today are the Soviet Union, Bulgaria, and Asia Minor. The *Rosa damascena* of ancient heritage is grown by these countries for their fragrant blooms from which oil (attar) of roses is extracted. It is said that five acres of these plants have to be grown to produce three tons of flowers, which in turn yield two and a half pounds of extract.

I hope this brief history of the rose entices you to search deeper into the subject.

# Roses to Tempt You

To have a garden filled with beautiful roses and vigorous, healthy bushes, you must buy the best available plants. Tending weak, non-productive roses is a waste of time and money.

Where to buy good roses is no problem, but before purchasing roses for your garden, you should have some knowledge of *how* to buy and of *what* you are buying.

In this country we are fortunate to have some of the greatest commercial rose growers and hybridizers in the world. These nurseries are constantly hybridizing and developing new varieties. You can buy directly from these growers and thus be assured of obtaining healthy plants of proven varieties.

The price of roses ranges from $1.50 to $3.50 per plant, rarely more, unless the rose offered for sale is a newly patented variety or the winner of some national or international award. Commercial roses are budded onto a vigorous understock and are rarely grown on their own roots. It takes the rose grower more than two years to develop the plant you buy. During this period the plant has to be fertilized, watered, kept disease-free, and advertised; often the expense includes replacement, if the plant does not produce. Roses, therefore, are not expensive. Where else can you make such a small investment and derive so much pleasure over a period of ten or more years?

## ஃ➤WHERE AND HOW TO BUY ROSES

Commercial rose growers publish beautiful catalogs twice a year to tempt us, and tempt us they do! In these catalogs you will find roses for any spot in the garden; roses that grow to any height from 4 inches to 30 feet and in every color of the artist's palette.

If you are a beginner, control your enthusiasm and buy only the number of bushes you can adequately tend. Start with not more than a dozen rose plants. When you understand the technique of growing roses, you can add to your collection. Buying a few new roses each year avoids cluttering the garden with varieties and colors you don't like and further stimulates your interest in roses.

My advice to beginners or even amateurs when they are studying catalogs and making their lists is to choose proven, well-known varieties, and then only the ones described as "disease-resistant."

Beginners should also realize that all roses are not suitable to all climates. Roses that grow luxuriant in Florida or California may not thrive in Maine, desert regions, or at high altitudes in Colorado. New varieties displayed at garden shows are always magnificent, but they were probably forced in greenhouses for the show. They rarely produce such quality or profusion of bloom when planted in the garden, where they are subject to the whims of the weather.

Request catalogs from several commercial nurseries or specialist growers, since they do not all propagate or sell the same varieties. Make your selection as early as possible and send your order promptly before the grower's stock is depleted. Be sure to state on the order sheet whether your roses are for fall or spring planting, and give the approximate date you wish to receive the plants. This information tells the grower when to make shipment. Your rose beds will have been prepared, and the roses can be planted as soon as they arrive. (*See List of Accredited Rose Growers, p. 151*).

## ᘒ&⊃ORDER ROSES FOR FALL OR SPRING PLANTING

Whether you plant your roses in the fall or in the spring is a matter of climate conditions and your own convenience. Wherever you live, before ordering your roses, consult with a local nurseryman on the best time to plant in your area.

### Fall vs. Spring Planting

In regions of the country where the ground does not freeze until late fall or early winter, fall planting may be preferable to spring planting. The earth is still warm from the summer sun, it is easily tilled, and the roses delivered for fall planting have been freshly dug at the nursery.

I find that roses planted in the fall develop more basal canes the following spring than do the same varieties planted in the spring. This is due primarily to the fact that these roses, freshly dug at the nursery, are still vigorous and begin to establish their roots, before the ground freezes.

Roses delivered for spring planting were dug at the nursery the previous fall and held in cool storage all winter. They are, therefore, not as vigorous as they were when freshly dug at the nursery and must be gotten into the ground as soon as possible after the ground thaws. If planted too late, the brilliant sun and warmth of early spring days encourages the development of top growth before the already shocked roots have time to establish their water conducting system in the soil. To protect the canes from drying, they must remain in the protective earth mound so long after planting that the bud union, not exposed to the warmth of the sun, is slow to develop basal canes.

In extremely cold areas of the country, spring planting may be necessary.  In warmer regions roses can be planted in early or mid-winter.

## ৯৯DIG THEM UP!

If at the end of a blooming season some roses are not compatible
with your color scheme, take them out, give them to a friend, and
replace them with colors more to your liking.
Some roses are tidy, others untidy, and drop their petals before the
entire bloom fades.  Catalogs omit this description.  When a variety
shows such bad habits in my garden, it is discarded and replaced
the following season.
Also, if some of your plants have been particularly susceptible to disease during the season, dig them out and burn them; these plants
show they do not like the area or may be of inferior stock.  Replace
them with plants of a different variety or purchase plants from another nursery.  Don't struggle to maintain them; they will never
give you any pleasure.

## ৯৯POTTED OR PACKAGED ROSE PLANTS

In the spring potted and packaged roses appear on sidewalks and store
counters all over town.  Don't be tempted to buy them — they may
have once been good plants, but I doubt that they were ever No. 1
grade stock.  Surely after having been packaged a long time and
left on sidewalks in the sun and wind or on counters in overheated
stores, they have dried out and their roots are injured before you
buy them.  They are certainly not worth the effort to plant, much
less tend.
If you must buy packaged roses to replace plants that have died

during the winter, buy only packages that carry the label of an *accredited rose nursery.* Potted roses are often old discards from some greenhouse. Beware of cheap mail order roses also!

## ᠔᠊THE AMERICAN ROSE SOCIETY

To increase your interest in roses, become a member of the American Rose Society. Membership in this organization will make you feel a part of the rosarian's world and add glamour to your new hobby.

Address: American Rose Society
4048 Roselea Place
Columbus, Ohio 43214

Membership entitles you to a monthly magazine, *The American Rose Annual,* and *Buying Guide for Roses.* The *Guide* is an invaluable service to beginners and experienced rosarians alike. The *Guide* gives the height, color, and performance-rating of roses under a National Rating System:

10 points, perfect rose (there are none!)
9 — 10 points, outstanding performance
8 — 8.9 points, excellent
7 — 7-9 points, good
6 — 6.9 points, fair

These ratings are compiled from reports sent in to the American Rose Society by members from all parts of the United States and Canada. Many varieties are not listed — this would be an unsurmountable task — but performance ratings of newly patented roses are being listed as soon as data can be evaluated.

Beginners or amateur rosarians should buy roses rated from 7.5 to 9 points. Then, when you have become experienced, you will have plenty of time to buy untried, new varieties. I have never seen a rose listed as having attained the full 10 points.

If you ask the American Rose Society, they will send you a list of roses that will help you make a wise choice.

## THE ROYAL NATIONAL ROSE SOCIETY

I urge you to become a member of The Royal National Rose Society of England. Articles by the great English scientist-rosarians are informative, stimulating, and give excellent, common-sense advice.

Address:  The Secretary
The Royal National Rose Society
Chiswell Green Lane
St. Albans, Herts, England

## MODERN GARDEN ROSES

Many rose books show pictures of modern roses and suggest roses for you to buy. I have purposely omitted this chapter, believing the beginner is confused by too many pictures and names of roses until he is familiar with their characteristics.
Roses in catalogs are listed as:

Hybrid Tea
Floribunda
Grandiflora
Polyantha
Miniature
Shrub
Ramblers

*Double Hybrid Tea*

### *Hybrid Teas* (HT)

The hybrid tea rose first appeared in 1867 and was created by cross-ing the vigorous Hybrid Perpetual with the China Tea rose, an ever-blooming hybrid imported from China to Europe in the 18th century. The hybrid tea is presently the most popular of all roses and is pro-pagated in almost every part of the world.

The buds of hybrid teas are long and pointed, and the flowers can be either fully double, semi-double, or single. Hybrid teas develop into bushes anywhere from 2 to 6 feet tall, depending on climate, the way you prune your bushes, and their food. Hybrid teas can be used for bedding in formal gardens or as shrubs in informal planting.

*Semi-double Hybrid Tea*

*Single Hybrid Tea*

*Floribunda* (FL) — Hybrid Polyantha

Floribundas are a relatively new type of rose (1924) developed by crossing Hybrid Teas with Polyanthas. These are among the most beautiful, prolific, and popular of the modern roses. They are of medium height, 2 to 3 feet, free-flowering with blossoms borne singly or in clusters, and they bloom continuously throughout the season. Floribunda roses can be used in front of taller growing varieties for bedding, low hedges, or wherever color is needed in the garden.

*Grandiflora* (Grfl)

Grandifloras are a cross between Hybrid Teas and Floribundas. They are vigorous, bloom continuously all summer, and bear blossoms singly or in clusters. Some varieties attain a height of 6 to 8 feet, if not pruned, and can be used as shrub roses.

*Polyantha Cluster*

*Polyantha* (Pol)

A bush, medium height, blooms all summer. Best used for mass planting and borders. The flowers are small, sometimes cupped, and

are usually borne in clusters.  Disease-resistant and hardy.  Polyanthas descend from the Japanese *Rosa multiflora* and a dwarf Chinese
rose.

All of the above described roses are available in myriads of colors
and for different purposes in the garden scheme as:

> Climbers
> Pillar or Shrub roses
> Tree or standard roses
> Weeping standards

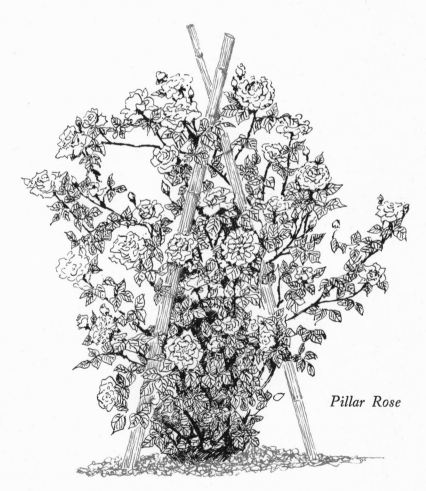

*Pillar Rose*

*Standard Tree Rose
and Miniature Rose*

### Climbers

Climbing roses do not actually climb as does a vine. They produce long supple canes that need some kind of support, such as fences or trellises, or they can be trained to fall or trail over walls. Some varieties bloom only in spring, while others are repeat bloomers. Removing fading flowers encourages some varieties to bloom again. Climbers need the same general care as hybrid teas, floribundas, or grandifloras, for some of the most popular of them are "sports" of the above mentioned varieties of the same name.

### Pillar or Shrub Roses

Pillar roses develop into plants 5 to 6 feet tall with strong canes, but most of them need some kind of support if trained as large shrubs. They make beautiful displays when tied to columns or pillars or trained on low rail fences and walls. They have large handsome blooms similar to the hybrid tea.

### Standard Tree Roses or Weeping Standards

These handsome accent roses stand regally on one strong cane 3 to 4 feet high crowned with a head of blooms. They are made by grafting any variety of hybrid tea, floribunda, grandiflora, or polyantha onto the top of a tall sturdy cane of an understock. Don't be afraid to use them. They are beautiful in the garden scheme and are not difficult to protect in winter.

### Miniature Roses

Miniature roses are not the runts of rosedom. They are a true rose that originally came from China. These little plants grow from 4 to 12 inches high, and their tiny buds and blossoms are as perfect as any hybrid tea. They are hardy in most climates and easy to care for. For real display, plant miniature roses in beds by themselves. Protect them from the wind by low hedges. Given the same care as hybrid teas, they will be covered from early spring to late fall with thousands of infinitesimal blooms in almost every color. They are a conversation piece and make a lovely children's garden.

*Ramblers* (Trailers)

This briar-type rose really rambles and is used to cover roadsides, slopes, and banks. They bloom once a season. Although ramblers are hardy, plant them with as much care as you would your garden rose. If you plant them on a slope, be sure to put down stones or something to hold the earth around the hole to prevent washing and exposure of roots.

## OLD, RARE, AND HISTORIC ROSES

When we think of roses in this modern age, we envision gardens filled with hybrid teas, floribundas, and grandiflora roses that bloom continuously all season. (Why, I wonder, is so much expected of the rose when other flowers and shrubs have only one burst of bloom!) Few people realize there are other glorious roses available that make equally magnificent displays in spring, while some bloom intermittently all summer.

These roses, known as old, rare, and historic, are vigorous growers, hardy and disease-resistant. They can be used in the garden scheme as bush roses, specimen shrubs, hedges, climbers, or trailers. Their exquisite blooms, whether single or double, differ in form from our popular garden roses and are intensely fragrant. Their leaves are decorative and also differ in form. The foliage of some varieties perfume the air when wet with dew or rain. In autumn, when the blooming season is over, many varieties are covered with colorful rose fruit (hips). One form of a species rose develops "shiny ebony-black hips" in the autumn.

Some rose enthusiasts collect these roses because of their fragrance, never considering the bloom or the plant's habits of growth. They are interested only in having their gardens filled with the perfume of roses, and designate their roses' various fragrances as cinnamon, tea, fruit, spice, musk, and one rose is even supposed to smell like beer.

A collection of rare, old, and historic roses can become a source of unique interest in your community and a conversation piece in your own garden.

Of the 200 known wild roses (botanical species), the most important ancestors of our modern roses are:

> R. gallica
> R. damascena
> R. moschata
> R. alba
> R. centifolia
> R. chinensis

I have given here a brief history of these roses and the names of others that you will encounter in books on old roses and in specialists' catalogs.

🐚GALLICA ROSES                                    *Rosa Gallica*

*R. Gallica* (Rosa Rubra)

This species rose is the illustrious ancestor of our present-day roses. In the 12th century B.C. it was the emblem of the Medes and the Persians and was extensively cultivated in the 4th century by the

Greeks. It most likely came to France and England with Roman settlers and is presumably the rose mentioned by Pliny in his treatise on gardening (23-79 A. D.).

### R. Gallica Officinalis

This rose is a semi-double mutation or "sport" of the R. gallica. Processed by the Greeks for medicinal purposes, it became famous in the 13th century in Provins, France, as the rose used in making powders, lotions, and ointments for indigestion, eye troubles, or skin irritation, and became known as the Apothecary's Rose and the Rose of Provins. In England this red rose captured the title of Red Rose of Lancaster when the Earl of Lancaster chose it as his emblem during the Wars of the Roses.

## DAMASK ROSES

### R. Damascena

A natural variation of the R. gallica. It is the important ancestor of most of our modern roses. Intensely fragrant, it has endowed our garden rose with its perfume. R. damascena has been identified as the rose in the beautiful murals in the Palace of Knossos in Crete, 2000 B. C. Brought to France from Damascus, it was named Rose of Damascus or Damask Rose, but had come to France many years earlier with Roman settlers.

### R. Damascena Bifera

This most famous of the Damask roses was cultivated by the Romans for its exquisite perfume and sold as a cut flower. Because of its tendency to bloom more than once a season, it was called the Autumn Damask or Four Seasons Rose. R. damascena bifera is available today from specialist rose growers.

### R. Damascena Trigintipetala

An intensely fragrant Damask is grown extensively in the Soviet Union, Bulgaria, and other countries for the purpose of extracting oil

*Rosa Damascena*

and attar of roses from its petals.

*R. Moschata* — (Musk Rose)

This species comes to us from the Middle East and the Himalayas, and was described by Pliny centuries ago. This wild species, if planted near a tree, will climb 30 to 40 feet up into the branches.

*R. Alba*

The White Rose of York is the earliest known hybrid. Noted for its beautiful foliage and pronounced scent, it was chosen by Richard Plantagenet, Duke of York, as his emblem during the Wars of the Roses. Later, when the two families of York and Lancaster were joined through a marriage, the emblem became a stylized red rose with a white rose superimposed in the center.

*R. Centifolia*

The Cabbage Rose or Rose of Provence is also known as the rose of a hundred petals. The term "cabbage" means form, not size, of this rose. Centifolia roses, as we know them today, were developed in Holland about 1700. Centifolias were favorites of the Dutch masters and can be identified in many of their paintings.

1. *Rosa Centifolia (Cabbage)*

2. *Rosa Chinensis*

1
—
2

### ᔷᔷCHINA ROSES (TEA)

### R. Chinensis

This garden rose had been cultivated in China for a thousand or more years before it was imported to Europe in the late 1700's. Brought from Bengal on ships that carried tea chests, it became known as the Tea or Bengal Rose, its scent supposedly resembling that of tea.

When crossed and hybridized with European roses, it gave its ever-blooming tendencies to our modern hybrids and its exquisite crimson coloring.

### R. Gigantea

This wild Chinese rose is native to the bush and jungle country of southern China and Burma, and grows 50 feet into trees.

### R. Odorata Ochroleuca

A yellow Chinese rose that arrived in England about 1824. Its descendants thrive best in warm climates.

## SOME INTERESTING SPECIES NATIVE TO VARIOUS COUNTRIES

### R. Banksiae (Lady Banks Rose)

In 1879 Joseph Banks introduced this native rose of China to Europe. Used as a climber or a rambler, it develops canes 30 or more feet long. The flowers are very fragrant and small. This rose grows luxuriantly in the south and in California.

### R. Californica

A shrub rose native to Western North America.

### R. Canina (Dog Rose)

A wild briar rose common to the woods of France and England. Acquired its name because the blooms and roots when processed in a special way were supposed to cure rabies. R. Canina is used in many areas as understock.

### R. Carolina (Pasture Rose)

A species rose native in this country from eastern Canada to the Gulf Coast.

### R. Eglanteria (Eglantine or Sweetbriar Rose)

An ancient species still popular in England. Is hardy anywhere.

Shakespeare mentions the apple-scented foliage of the Eglantine Rose in his "A Midsummer-Night's Dream".

*R. Hugonis* (Golden Rose of China)

Was discovered in China by the French missionary, Father Hugo, and sent to Europe. A spreading shrub 6 feet high and wide, this beautiful rose has fern-like foliage and single bright yellow flowers. Lovely in any shrub garden.

*R. Laevigata* (Cherokee Rose)

This popular rose, now the state flower of Georgia, is not an American species but a native of China. Cherokee roses thrive all through the south, but are not hardy in colder regions of this country.

*Moss Roses*

Moss roses are mutations or "sports" of the *R. centifolia*. These lovely and fragrant roses were popular during the 18th century. Some varieties are available today.

*R. Multiflora* (R. Polyantha)

A vigorous climbing species from Japan. Used extensively by rose growers as understock for garden roses. Gives extra vigor to the variety budded on it. When this rose is established as a hedge, it becomes so thick and dense that it is now being used as a crash barrier on some highways. It is said a car traveling at 30 to 50 miles an hour will come to a gentle stop without serious injury to the car or passengers when it encounters this natural barrier.

*R. Rugosa*

Comes from Japan. Hardy anywhere in any soil, it is particularly hardy at the seashore. The hips of this rose are the ones that are so rich in Vitamin C.

*R. Setigera* (Prairie Rose)

A native species in this country, is hardy from Canada to Florida.

*R. Soulieana*

A vigorous spreading plant native to western China, was sent to Europe in 1896 by Father Souli. This marvelous spreading plant with exquisite foliage and white flowers is still available from specialist growers.

### R. Spinosissima

The Scotch Briar or Burnett rose grows wild on the sand dunes of the coast of Great Britain. Crossed with hybrid teas, this strain has helped to produce some of the most beautiful and useful of our hybrids and shrub roses.

### R. Spinosissima Altaica

This Asiatic form comes from the Altai Mountains in Siberia and develops "shiny, ebony-black" seeds or hips.

### R. Virginiana

A species shrub native to eastern North America. This small shrub is densely foliaged and has pink, single flowers. The bright green foliage in fall turns to autumn colors.

### R. Wichuriana

Often called the Memorial Rose. Excellent ground cover for holding banks. Has single white flowers with yellow stamen and blooms only in the spring. Left unpruned, it develops beautiful red hips for fall display. Its canes will take root if covered with soil.

To further interest you in species, hybrid shrubs, and climbing roses, I urge you to read the following books on the subject by some of my favorite authors:

Dorothy Stemler, "The Book of Old Roses"
Richard Thomson, "Old Roses for Modern Gardens"
Graham Stuart Thomas, "Climbing Roses Old and New"
        and "Shrub Roses of Today"
F. Fairbrother, "Roses"
Bertram Park, "The Guide to Roses" and
        "The World of Roses"
Francis E. Lester, "My Friend the Rose"
Helen Van Pelt Wilson, "Climbing Roses"

# Choose the Planting Area with Care

Roses will grow almost anywhere in the garden except in dense shade, but they want a permanent place where they can develop a sturdy root system. If you choose the planting area with care and take the trouble to properly prepare the bed, they will pay you royal dividends for years to come.

## ROSES HAVE DEFINITE LIKES AND DISLIKES

They like to be:
> Fertilized
> Watered
> Pruned
> Mulched
> Disease free
> Pest free
> and *Loved!*

*Roses dislike being crowded*, so consider the proximity of the rose bed to buildings, garden walls, and hedges.

*Good air-circulation* (micro-climate) is of utmost importance. Roses planted in gardens enclosed by high hedges or walls are more susceptible to disease and insect attacks than roses planted where the air-flow is good. However, the constant winds of summer and winter gales are equally bad.

*Roses need* 6 *to* 8 *hours of sun a day*, preferably morning sun, to dry the dew and thus minimize the development of the fungus spores of blackspot, mildew, and rust. In climates where the sun is intense, some afternoon shade is important to help blooms maintain color and to protect their canes from drying.

*Root thieves* (roots of trees, shrubs, grass, and border plants) must not be allowed to encroach on the rose bed. They steal nourishment put in the soil to benefit the roses.

*Grass* is a dreadful food thief, so twice a year cut the grass by edging the beds to the full depth of a sharp spade. There are several types of metal edgings for flower beds that can be buried below ground level to control grass roots.

*Boxwood edgings* are popular, but boxwood is a vigorous plant. It develops a dense root system that will, after a few years, deprive the rose of food. Furthermore, when the boxwood hedge has to be trimmed and clippings cover the mulch, you will have a real clean-up job.

*Perennials and annuals* — sometimes used as border plants or ground cover — may be lovely for a time, but when their flowers begin to fade, they detract from the neatness of the rose bed, and this usually occurs just as the roses are coming into their beautiful autumn bloom. Furthermore, they steal nutrients from the rose.
Caution:

*Edible plants* (such as lettuce or parsley) should never be used to edge rose beds; for the chemicals used to control rose pests and diseases are detrimental to humans.


ॐ➤MAKE A PLAN BEFORE YOU ORDER YOUR ROSES


When designing your rose beds, make a plan. Carefully note the location of each rose and use this plan as your guide when you plant.

Careful spacing of plants is important, for although roses like the tips of their leaves to touch and shade the ground underneath, they also like space for their roots to develop without intertwining in their neighbors' roots.

*The easiest bed* to care for is the one you can approach from both sides.

Example:

|  two-row bed  |  three-row bed  |
|:---:|:---:|
| X  X  X  X  X  X  X | X  X  X  X  X  X |
|  | X  X  X  X  X  X  X |
| X  X  X  X  X  X  X | X  X  X  X  X  X |

Stagger your plants in alternating rows. An area 4 feet by 12 feet will take a dozen average size plants. Allow 8 to 10 inches from the edge of the bed to the center of the bush. The distance between plants is measured from bud union to bud union.

The bud union is the enlarged knot at the top of the shank, above the roots. This is the area where the basal canes develop. The bud union is created by grafting (budding) any rose variety on to a cane of a fast-growng, sturdy understock. When the bud develops into a strong plant, the understock is cut away, leaving the swollen area called the bud union.

Recommended spacing:

| | |
|---|---|
| Grandifloras | 24 to 30 inches |
| Hybrid Teas | 22 to 24 inches |
| Floribundas | 20 to 22 inches |
| Polyanthas | 18 to 20 inches |
| Miniatures | 6 to 12 inches |
| Climbers or Pillar Roses | 6 feet or more |
| Shrubs | 4 feet or more |

Remember, roses planted in warm regions develop into much larger bushes than the same variety planted in a colder climate; therefore, judge your planting distance according to the region in which you live. Order only the number of bushes indicated by your plan.

# The Good Earth

If the roses you buy are to thrive, develop strong canes and healthy leaves, and produce beautiful bloom, plant them in well-prepared rose beds. But before preparing your rose beds, it is well to understand four important factors that govern rose culture:

> Soil
> Humus (organic matter)
> pH
> Drainage

When I started growing roses, I thought soil was just earth and that it was either good or bad. If it was bad, the gardener added some manure, and that was it. Furthermore, I supposed that soil and loam were one and the same. After a while I also learned that a material called *humus* is *not soil* at all, even though it looks like it.

Now that I know the difference, I find the subject so fascinating I am giving you information I wish someone had given me years ago.

ह∾SOIL

According to the encyclopedia, soil is the "upper layer of the earth that may be dug or plowed; specifically, the loose surface material in which plants grow." *Soil* has been built up through the centuries by decomposing animal and plant life, and lies on top of stones, shale, and rocks. It is the *basic ingredient* used in the preparation of rose beds, and is the top layer of earth in your own garden.

This layer of topsoil is classified as:

> Loam soil
> Sand soil
> Clay soil

It is rare that native soil cannot be used or improved for use in the rose bed, so don't order topsoil until you evaluate your own.

*How to Evaluate Soil*

Texture and color are the clues to your soil's usability. To determine the type of soil you have to work with in your area, remove the grass sod and dig a spadeful of earth in several places in your proposed rose garden.

Good soil is dark brown to black in color, breaks into clumps when dug, and crushes easily when handled. Soil of this texture is porous (friable) and according to the dictionary is "full of holes through which fluid, air, and light may pass." This is the structure we strive so hard to achieve for rose culture.

*Loam Soil*: (color dark to light brown)

Loam, a combination of sand, clay, and humus (organic matter) is the best and most fertile soil for use in rose beds. It is porous, provides good drainage and aeration, but has moisture-holding capabilities so vital to rose growth and health.

*Sandy Soil*: (color, brown to sand color)

Light textured sandy soils cannot hold moisture. Water flows freely through the grains, by-passes thirsty roots, and leaches valuable foods from the soil. To improve the texture and increase the moisture-holding capacity of sandy soils, add *peat moss* in generous amounts. To increase the bacterial content of any soil, add humus of any kind plus manure. Improved sandy soil grows very fine roses.

*Clay Soil*: (color, yellow to red)

Texture is compact, sticks to the spade when dug, and will not crumble. Clay soils hold *too much moisture* and become boggy in rainy seasons. Coarse sand plus humus are needed in generous amounts to make this soil friable. Clay soils are usually rich in potash, so roses planted in improved clay soils display brilliant color in their blooms and develop healthy foliage.

*Fill*:

The worst soil to work with is "fill" found around newly-built houses. This material is well named for it is literally filled with cement, nails, bits of board, paper, and often rocks hauled in from someone's excavated cellar. After a bulldozer has dozed it several times, it becomes an impenetrable structure known as hardpan. Nothing can grow in this mess. *Dig it out*, bring in topsoil from another area and fill the rose beds to a depth of twenty-four to thirty-six inches with soil that has been well mixed with humus.

## HUMUS (ORGANIC MATTER)

Humus is *decaying plant life* and animal refuse. The decaying process is carried on by bacteria and earthworms that live and die in the soil, but when the *decaying process stops*, the material is no longer humus. It becomes just soil, and its value as a conditioning agent ends. It is important, therefore, to add humus to the rose bed each spring to keep the decaying process constant in the soil.

Humus is the *most important of all materials* to add to soil when preparing a rose bed and may be used in any quantity or combinations needed to develop friable soil. Humus mixed with native soil changes and improves texture. Water and rain pass freely through the pores, the soil is thus aerated, oxygen reaches plant roots, and bacterial growth is encouraged. Because of its spongy quality, humus holds moisture in proper balance, thereby deterring leaching of nutrients.

*Available Sources of Humus are*:

Compost
Leaf mold
Peat
Seaweed
Manure (cow - sheep)
Mushroom manure

*Compost* — is the result of carefully controlled decomposition of vegetable matter in which bacterial activity and earthworms are encouraged. Compost is not just a haphazard mess of decomposing rubbish. When correctly made, compost creates an excellent humus and organic food.

*Leaf mold* — that thin layer of decomposed plant life, rich in organic matter, found under leaves in heavily wooded areas. Save autumn leaves, pile them in a selected area where they can rot, and in a few years you will have your own leaf mold. Oak leaves and pine needles are more acid in reaction than other kinds of leaves.

*Peat* — decomposed vegetable and animal refuse accumulated over hundreds of years in bogs and marshes under practically airless conditions. Peat is spongy, holds moisture, and by its texture creates a friable soil. Use in combination with compost, leaf mold or manure. Peat has no nutritive value, so use as a *soil conditioner* only. Peat has a high acid reaction.

*Seaweed* — dried and shredded. Available at the seashore. Excellent organic material. High bacterial content.

*Manure* — the primary function of animal manures is to add live bacteria and earthworms to the soil and improve texture. Manures are low in nutritive value.

*Mushroom manure* — not generally recommended for use in rose beds. However, one great California rosarian uses 'spent" mushrooms as a fertilizer.

## ஃ⊸TEST YOUR SOIL

Now that you have some understanding of the ingredients needed to make native soil usable and fertile, you must have positive knowledge of how much of any material or element is needed to bring your garden soil to the roses' requirements, and whether your soil is acid or alkaline. A complete soil analysis will give you this information.

So, before buying materials to incorporate into the soil, save time and money by sending soil samples to your State Agricultural Station or Agricultural College for analysis. Usually these tests are free of charge. This analysis will describe soil texture, approximate amounts of nitrogen, phosphorous, potash, and iron present, and will give the pH (acidity or alkalinity) rating of the soil.

Soil tests should be made twice a year, first in early spring before feeding, and again in mid-summer to determine soil conditions. When the report is received, take it to your garden supply company specialist or nurseryman, have him interpret the recommendations, and advise you on what materials are best to use in your vicinity and how much per square foot to apply to meet the soil's requirements. Not only is this the safest method, but it will increase your interest as well as knowledge.

You can do some of the tests yourself if you buy a Sudbury Soil Test Kit. Testing soil is fun and adds zest to mixing fertilizers.

*How To Take Soil Samples*

1. Take a small trowel of soil from several spots in the proposed rose bed.
2. Mix soil and dry naturally.

3. Place soil in cartons, seal tightly, and mail.

Be sure to mention the tests are for roses, or you'll get information on how to grow vegetables!

*Town or Well Water*

It is important to know the alkaline content of the water used for roses. Ask your local Board of Health for an analysis of the town water. If you use well water, have it tested too. If the water you are using is alkaline, it is best to be aware of it so you can intelligently cope with your rose problems.

৪৯PH

pH refers to the acidity or alkalinity (lime content) of soil and is expressed in a table of values. Neutral is 7.0. Any numeral above 7.0 is progressively alkaline (sweet), any number below 7.0 is increasingly acid (sour).

Roses prefer a pH of 5.5 to 6.5, never higher. Roses will not thrive in an alkaline media.

*Never attempt to change* the pH condition of your soil unless you know exactly what you are doing, or you'll get into trouble with Mother Nature.

*Acid Soil*

When your soil test shows an acid rating (pH 5.0 or lower), raise the pH to the roses' required rating of 5.5 or slightly higher by using one of the following conditioners:

> Ground limestone (agricultural lime)
> Dolomitic limestone
> Hydrated lime
> Crushed oyster shells

Lime, when in proper proportion in the soil, serves many important functions. It not only corrects acidity, but helps in changing the soil's structure by hastening bacterial action. Lime aids in the liberation of plant foods that would otherwise remain in unavailable form in the soil and encourages decomposition of organic matter. Some limestone supplies small amounts of trace elements, such as calcium and magnesium, which are often deficient in native soil.

*When correcting an acid soil condition*, don't add all the required lime at one time. It is safer and easier to add a little at a time than to try to counteract an excess later. Remember, lime in correct proportion in the soil serves many purposes, but overliming "locks" some important nutrients in the soil, making them unavailable to plant roots. Caution:

Lime must be applied to the rose bed six weeks (longer, if possible) before planting your roses. Use lime by itself. Do not mix lime with nitrogenous fertilizers or animal manures for application to the soil.

### How to Apply Limestone

Spread lime evenly over the surface of the bed, work carefully into the top inch or so of the soil, and water well.

1. *Ground limestone* (agricultural lime) is the safest product for amateurs to use. A light sprinkling over small areas is usually sufficient to "sweeten" the soil unless your professional soil analysis calls for heavier liming.

2. *Dolomitic limestone* is good to use in soil that needs periodic liming. Dolomitic lime has magnesium present. Use only as directed by a professional gardener or specialist.

3. *Hydrated lime* may be used, but ground limestone is safer and has a more lasting effect than quick-acting, hydrated lime.

4. *Crushed oyster shells* are safe to use when available.

### Alkaline Soil

Lower the pH from alkaline to slightly acid (6.5) by using: *Powdered Sulphur* — use only as directed by your professional soil analysis.

### Slightly Alkaline Soil

If the pH is only slightly alkaline, the soil may be brought to the proper rating by the addition of organic matter.

*Peat Moss* (sphagnum) has an acid reaction and can be used in generous amounts if needed to acidify soil in established rose beds. Cover the beds with one to two inches of sphagnum peat and carefully work it into the soil. Water well.

## ᘐ DRAINAGE

Adequate drainage in a rose bed is of utmost importance. Water and rainfall must permeate the soil and subsoil freely, but must never become stagnant or pool in the lower segment of the bed. Roses will not tolerate wet feet.

When evaluating drainage conditions in your garden, keep in mind the fact that drainage must not only take care of regular watering and rainfall, but also deal with excessive amounts of moisture during long, rainy seasons and melting spring snow.

### To Determine Drainage

Dig a hole 18 to 24 inches deep. Fill the hole with water; if the water drains off in three or four hours, the drainage is probably good, but if it stands in the hole for a longer time, proper drainage must be created. Drainage is necessary to a depth of:

24 inches in friable or sandy soils,
36 inches or more in heavy or clay soils.

*Poor drainage* can be improved in several ways, but regardless of the method used, remove all soil to a depth of 36 inches before attempting to correct the problem.

If you have a serious drainage problem, I advise you to confer with a landscape gardener or contractor. Artificial drainage is very expensive, and unless done correctly, will be of no use to the rose.

However, if you insist on doing the job yourself, here are a few suggestions:

1.   Dig a trench 36 inches deep. Make sure there is a good run-off to a lower level of the garden. Then lay four-inch agricultural *tiles* end to end, and *cover* the joints with tar paper to prevent soil from seeping in.

2. Gravel or small stones placed approximately 8 inches deep on the bottom of the trench or hole will also create good drainage if the problem is not serious.

## ⁖►PREPARE THE ROSE BED PROPERLY

By now you know how to determine the soil's needs and what conditioners to use, so you are on your own. But remember, nothing you add to the surface soil, once your roses are planted, will give the results of carefully prepared subsoil, for it is here that the rose establishes its roots .

Digging any flower bed is a man's job, and rose beds are no exception. If you are smart, you will engage the services of a man who likes to dig (if you can find one), for it takes stamina and brawn to prepare a bed deep enough for adequate drainage and then refill the trench or hole with well-mixed soil.

Prepare the beds months or weeks before planting to allow for settling. When roses are planted in freshly made beds, the bud union is apt to settle below the desired ground level. Preparation will be easier if you have all needed ingredients and tools handy before starting the beds.

*Some helpful hints*

You will need:

> Canvas squares or sacking on which to save topsoil.
> Two wheelbarrows to haul away earth, shale, and rocks.
> Spades
> Fork
> Peat (sphagnum)
> Leaf mold, compost, or both
> Bone Meal
> Blood Meal
> Fish Meal

*Some Advice*

Manure may be added to the soil mixture if the beds are being prepared *months before planting time*. But, if your beds are being prepared for almost immediate planting, do not add manures or chemical (inorganic) fertilizers. The plant, having been shocked by handling, does not need these fertilizers until the root system has time to become established. Nitrogen is particularly undesirable at this time. Newly planted roses rapidly develop tiny feeding roots after being set in the ground. Strong fertilizers burn these important little roots, and the plant dies.

*In late spring* after growth and leaves are fully developed, you can then apply a liquid plant food, such as Atlas Fish Emulsion, Rapid-Gro, Ortho Liquid Rose Food, or any other well-balanced liquid food, as a stimulant. Or you can apply a dry commercial rose food formula to the surface, one-half cup per plant. (*See Feeding Established Roses, p. 78*).

Because it is difficult for the beginner to estimate the amount of humus needed to condition native soil and change the texture, or how much organic food to incorporate when making new beds, here is help.

*Depending on your soil analysis and soil texture*, using a bucket as your measure, mix with:

*Loam Soil*

Peat — 1 bucket to 3 buckets of soil
Bone Meal — 1 cup per plant
Blood Meal or Fish Meal — ½ cup per plant

*Sandy Soil*

Never add loam to improve sandy soil. It will only make the problem worse.
Peat — 1 bucket to 1 bucket of soil (half and half)
Leaf mold or compost — ½ bucket
Bone Meal — 1 cup per plant
Blood Meal or Fish Meal — ½ cup per plant

*Clay Soil*

Peat — 1 bucket to 2 buckets of soil. Add a small amount of coarse

sand to help break the compact clay texture and make the soil friable.
Leaf mold or compost — ½ bucket
Bone Meal — 1 cup per plant
Blood Meal or Fish Meal — ½ cup per plant

*Now you're ready for work*

1. Remove the sod, put it in a corner of the garden to decompose for use elswhere.
2. Next, remove 6 to 8 inches of topsoil, place on canvas to be mixed with peat, etc.
3. Dig 20 to 30 inches deep depending on drainage needs.
4. Remove all rocks and don't be careless! Discard all useless material.

*Layering*

The easiest way to fill a trench or hole is to add all ingredients in layers, turning with a fork as you add to insure a good mixture.
1. Fill the bottom of the trench with 6 to 8 inches of soil.
2. Add 2 to 3 inches of peat as needed to change or improve texture. Leaf mold or compost may also be added.
3. Now spread a generous cover of bone meal and a thin sprinkling of blood meal or fish meal and fork these layers to mix thoroughly.
4. Continue adding ingredients layer by layer until the bed is almost ground level.
5. Add 2 inches of manure (well rotted) to the top few inches of the bed, never lower. If cow manure is not available, you can substitute composted cow or sheep manure and use as directed on the package. Mix thoroughly and let the earth fallow several weeks to allow for settling.

# The Roses Arrive

When a plant is dug for shipment, its roots have to be drastically cut and are often broken. The canes too are pruned back to probably one-half their original height. The grower ships these roses bare-rooted (without earth on the roots). Having been en route several days, the canes and roots may have dried out and need your immediate attention. They are in surgical shock. It will take infinite care to revive these plants and encourage the little roots to begin growth again.

If your plants arrive packaged in polyethylene bags, you're lucky — the canes will be moist and in good condition.

Nevertheless:

1.  Open the bag, examine the roots and canes.
2.  If they are moist, close the bag tightly and return the bag to the carton.
3.  Store in a cool, dark place until you are ready to plant. The stor-

age area temperature should never go below 32 degrees nor above 50 degrees F.

Some growers ship roses packed in wet moss and wrapped in paper. These plants will either be dry or slimy wet.

1. Remove and discard all wrappings.

2. Immerse the entire plant in water regardless of its condition (dry or slimy).

3. Drain and rewrap in some type of polyethylene cover. Store as directed above and hold for planting.

ROSES ARRIVE FOR SPRING PLANTING

Spring planting must be done as soon as possible after the ground thaws and no later than April 15. If roses are planted late in the spring, the warm earth and sun stimulate top growth before the roots, shocked by handling and exposure, have time to establish themselves well enough to take on the responsibility of furnishing food for the new growth.

*Delayed Spring Planting*

If weather or circumstances delays planting longer than two or three days after the arrival of your roses:

1. Dig a trench 10 or 12 inches deep in the rose bed, long enough to accommodate all the roots. Save all soil for reuse.

2. Carefully separate the bushes and place the roots in the trench.

3. Cover the plant with soil removed from the trench to within a few inches of the top of the canes.

4. Wet the soil. Planting can now be delayed one week — no longer.

ROSES ARRIVE FOR FALL PLANTING

When your order is received in the fall, have a look at your plants and get them into the ground as soon as possible, for an early snow or hard freeze can make planting practically impossible.

### Delayed Fall Planting

When planting has to be delayed, I advise you to *completely bury* your plants. The roses will be safe all winter; when spring comes and all danger of freezing has passed, you can dig your roses and plant them. They will have had a good winter's rest.

### To Bury Rose Plants:

1.  Remove enough soil from the rose bed to make a trench 12 or 14 inches deep. Place soil on a canvas for reuse.
2.  Carefully separate your plants, lay them side by side in the trench, and cover with a light dusting of soil.
3.  Next, cover the roses with wire hardware cloth, available in several widths at any good hardware store. The wire cloth cover will protect your plants from field mice and moles, and will make digging easier and safer in the spring.
4.  Cover the hardware cloth with soil removed from the bed. Then fill the trench to several inches above ground level.
5.  Keep the earth moist until the ground freezes.
6.  In very cold regions cover the entire area with boughs and leaves for extra protection.

### GETTING READY TO PLANT

If the day is good, (not too cold or windy) gather your tools and get to work. You will need the following equipment:

> Rake
> Spade — pointed
> Fork
> Trowel
> Stakes — one for each rose to be planted.
>> (Green bamboo stakes are good.)
> Yard stick — to measure distances between plants.

Heavy cord — to run the length of the bed to keep bushes
in line.
Pruning shears — clean and sharp.
Knife — clean and sharp.
Garden gloves — you'll need them!
Watering hose
Bucket or pail
Basket — for debris

An interested helper makes planting easier.

1. Rake, clean, and level the beds.

2. Carefully measure the distance between plants as indicated by
your plan and place a stake firmly in the spot where each rose is to
be planted. (Stringing a cord the length of the bed will help to keep
them in line.)

3. Fill a wheelbarrow or tub with water (muddy water is best).

4. Carefully remove your roses from their wrappings or trench and
place their roots in the water.

5. Cover the container with sacks or what-have-you, and keep them
out of the sun and wind while you prepare the holes. Roses can be
seriously injured if their canes or roots dry out before planting.

*Lines run to show the position of each bush*

*Waiting to be planted*

ஃ PLANTING DIRECTIONS

After a bush is planted and the soil has settled, the bud union should be slightly above ground level. Keep this in mind while planting.

1. Remove the soil around each stake where a rose is to be planted and place the soil on a canvas for reuse.

2. Prepare each hole 18 inches deep and approximately 20 inches in diameter.

3. Next, make a small, firm cone in the center of the hole on which to set the plant.

4. When several holes have been prepared, take one plant at a time from the water container. Note the shape of the plant, and cut off any broken roots. Never sacrifice any part of a healthy root. Be thankful for every inch the grower spared you.

5. Gently open the roots and set the plant on the cone. Never twist or turn under the roots. Make the hole to fit the individual plant. Another caution, don't try forcing open the big roots or pushing the plant into the hole. These big roots act like springs and will push the plant upward above the desired ground level several days, even weeks, after planting.

6. Check the level by placing a stick across the bed at the bud union. Adjust your plant until it is at the correct level. Hold the plant steady and add soil a little at a time. Gently press the soil in and around the roots and crown to hold the plant firmly in place. When the hole is about two-thirds full, tamp the earth with your feet.

7. Fill the hole with water to remove air pockets. When the water drains off, fill the hole with soil to an inch or so above ground level. This extra soil allows for settling.

8. Hold your rose at the correct level, and again press or gently tamp the soil.

9. The bud union should now have settled to just at or above ground level; if the bud union has settled below the desired level, do not drag the plant upward. Dig carefully, and reset.

These planting instructions may sound complicated. — they are not.

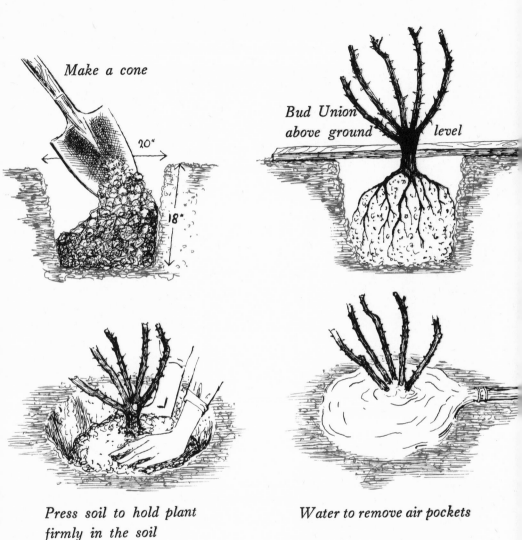

*Make a cone*

*Bud Union above ground level*

*Press soil to hold plant firmly in the soil*

*Water to remove air pockets*

Actually, after you have planted a few bushes, I am sure you will agree it is the best and quickest way to plant roses in a private garden.

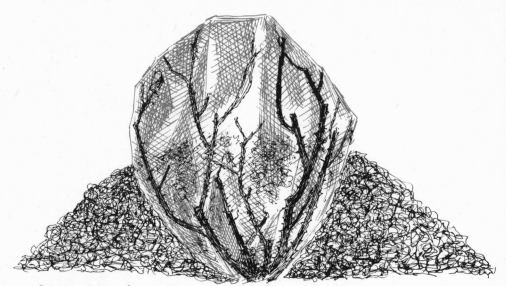

*Green plastic bag with protective earth mound*

## PROTECT ROSES PLANTED IN SPRING

The next step is to protect your newly planted bushes. *Their canes must not be allowed to dry out.* To prevent drying and to protect them from wind, sun, or rapid changes of temperatures, cover the canes of each plant with a plastic bag (these bags are now available in green and are less conspicuous than white covers). Mound soil over the plastic bag, up and around the canes, to a height of 8 to 10 inches. Do not add boughs or leaves at spring planting time.

### *When to Remove Protective Mounds and Plastic Bags*

It is difficult to tell you when to remove the protective plastic bags and earth mounds. My best advice is to leave all protection on the plants until new shoots within the bag are 2 to 3 inches long. In many regions, the sunny warm days of early spring encourage the gardener to start this job too soon. It must be remembered that the warm spring days in April are often followed by nights with temperatures that drop into the low thirties. Nothing is more destructive to newly planted bushes than drastic changes of temperature. Such rapid temperature shifts injure unprotected new shoots. Watch the weather reports and be guided by them before removing the protective covering.

*Some Hints on Removing Mounds and Plastic Bags*

1. Be wise. Do not remove all the earth mound and the plastic bag the same day. New shoots, having been warm and protected within their cover, should not be subjected to the elements too abruptly. Remove part of the mound; then a day or two later, after the plants have become adjusted, remove the plastic bag and use a gentle spray from a water hose to remove the soil packed in and around the canes and bud union. Rinsing away the soil precludes the chance of breaking off valuable young shoots.
2. Prune any dead wood or dieback.
3. Remove any nameplate tied to canes with wire. The wire may kill the cane if left on for any length of time. Re-label the bush. You will enjoy being able to identify each rose.
4. Clean and rake the beds.
5. Now, spread a good mulch over the entire bed.
(*See Mulching, pp. 61-65*)

*Never feed newly planted roses.* If you have followed directions for rose bed preparation, there will be enough food in the soil to take care of the roses' needs until the leaves are fully developed and the buds showing color. (*See Feeding Established Roses, p. 78*).

&PROTECT ROSES PLANTED IN FALL

Roses planted in fall need protection from winter sun and whipping winds. Actually, they are safer under a solid blanket of snow all winter than they are when exposed to the whims of the weather and alternating thaws and freezes.

1. Mound each bush with light soil well up into the canes.

2. Firm the mounds to prevent heaving.

3. If available, fill the valleys around the hillocks with well-rotted manure or humus of some kind to keep the earth warm and prevent erosion.

4. Cover the entire bed lightly with evergreen boughs. In spring remove earth mounds as directed.

Remember to feed these roses in spring when the foliage is fully developed and the buds are showing color.

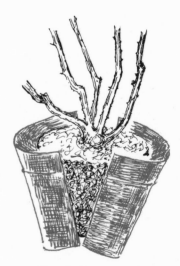

*Cut container*                    *Carefully remove cover*

## PLANTING POTTED OR PACKAGED ROSES

Roses bought in cartons or tins should be planted as soon as possible after buying. When you bought them, they had probably been potted or packaged too long, and may have been injured by drying out in the container.

### To Plant Packaged Roses

Do not disturb the roots of potted or packaged roses. Prepare the soil as for bare-rooted roses. Dig a hole to fit their container, gently remove the pot, tar paper, or tin, and place the plant intact in the well-prepared soil. Firm the earth around the roots. Mix 2 table-spoons of Rapid-Gro in a 2½ gallon pail of water, and pour over the soil. When the water drains away, fill the hole to the ground level with prepared soil.

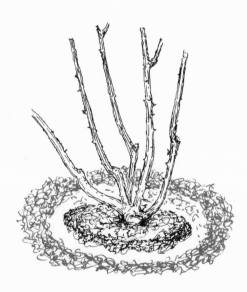

*Place in hole,
tamp soil —
and water*

### TRANSPLANTING ROSES

When roses are to be moved from one place in the garden to another, it is best to move them when they are dormant, in early spring or in late fall after they have shed their leaves.

1.  Prepare the hole long enough before transplanting to allow the soil to settle.

2.  Prune canes back to 18 inches or 24 inches.

3.  Wet the soil the day before transplanting.

4.  Dig the bush carefully and keep a good earth ball on your plant. Protect the roots with plastic or sacking while moving. Gently place the plant in the hole. (*See Protect Roses Planted in Spring, p. 56*).

# Mulches

Mulching means to cover the earth with any light material that spreads easily and holds moisture. Mulches are used for specific purposes and are most important to the health of a rose plant.

1. Mulching keeps the beds *weed-free*.
2. A good, light-textured mulch *holds moisture, prevents evaporation*, and thus keeps roots moist and cool in hot, dry weather. Tests show the soil temperature under a mulch to be 10 to 20 degrees F. cooler than the temperature of the soil in beds not mulched.
3. A good mulch makes *watering easy;* for as water is applied the mulch lifts, and the flow of water is directed evenly throughout the bed.
4. Mulching *prevents baking* or *crusting* of the topsoil. This is important; for when the top layer of the bed hardens, cultivation of the soil becomes necessary to allow water to penetrate to the thirsty roots and to aerate the soil. Cultivation, unless very carefully done, can do more harm than good, because too often tools used to loosen soil cut or injure the plant's superficial roots.
5. Mulching *prevents soil erosion* during heavy rainfall or watering.
6. The most important function performed by the mulch is to

*prevent soil from splattering* onto the lower canes and leaves of the bush during rainfall or watering. *Soil splatter must be prevented;* the reason being that fungus spores attack only when the soil and plant are wet. For instance, should a leaf infected with the fungus spore of blackspot from the previous season be left to rot *in* or *on* the ground, that leaf remains a potential source of infection until it has completely disintegrated. A good mulch that protects the bush from soil splatter, therefore, lessens the chance of fungus infection. From experience I am convinced that mulching is the practical and best way to control blackspot. (*See Diseases, p. 95*).

Caution:
If the rose bushes have been infected with any rose fungus problem during the summer, remove and burn all *mulch and dead leaves* from the bed before applying protective winter mounds. *Do not add the debris to your compost pile.*


༄MULCHES (ORGANIC)


For your convenience I have listed here the best and most commonly used organic materials with which to mulch your rose beds; buckwheat hulls, cocoa bean hulls, ground tree bark, peat moss, cow manure, compost, ground leaves, ground corn cobs, straw, grass clippings, seaweed, pine needles, sawdust.

The first three mulches, in the order listed, *buckwheat hulls, cocoa bean hulls,* and *ground tree bark* (all commercially available), are my personal choice for use in private gardens. Rose beds covered with any of these are not only lovely to look at but are easy to tend; these mulches are not expensive, if you take into account the hours of work they save the gardener and the protection they give the rose bush.

*Buckwheat hulls* — commercially available; sold under the trade names, Multex or Protecto. Rich brown in color, the hulls are light in texture but will not blow away in windy weather. If buckwheat hulls are not available in your locality, ask your garden supply company to order the product for you.

*Cocoa bean hulls* — commercial product; trade name Ko-K-O. A dark brown color, somewhat coarser in texture than buckwheat hulls. Cocoa bean hulls deteriorate into a good material to incorporate into the soil at the end of the season. Has an odor of cocoa for a few days after being applied. Cocoa bean hulls tend to pack and shed water unless stirred often. Other cocoa bean hull products are also available.

*Ground tree bark* — commercially available; (a paper mill product). Dark brown color, coarse textured like shredded sphagnum moss, slightly acid.

*Peat moss* — commercially available. Sphagnum peat is best for rose beds. Light brown color, slightly acid, peat may steal nitrogen from the soil. Peat moss should be incorporated into the soil when the beds are prepared, and not used as a mulch, for after being on the beds awhile, peat cakes, hardens, and makes water-penetration of the soil practically impossible. Peat moss has been used *unwisely as a mulch* for too many years.

*Cow manure* — not readily available. Manure is best used incorporated into the soil when preparing the bed. I do not like to see manure used as a mulch in private gardens for it is smelly and unsightly. Furthermore, in some regions, it tends to keep the canes hot and moist, causing rot. (*See The Roses' Diet, p. 77*).

*Compost* — when good commercial mulches are not available, well-rotted, sifted compost makes an excellent substitute. It adds bacteria and trace elements to the soil.

*Ground leaves* — good humus to incorporate into the bed — use as a *substitute* mulch only. Never use leaves unless they are finely ground. Leaves are apt to keep the canes too moist, thereby causing cane rot. Leaves, if not ground or rotted, deter penetration of water to the roots.

*Ground corncobs* — inexpensive in certain areas, are not a good color, may stay wet and rot canes. While decomposing, ground corncobs steal nitrogen from the soil.

*Straw* — unslightly, steals nitrogen from the soil while decomposing. Straw is preferably used as a winter mulch but is difficult to remove.

*Grass clippings* — never use as a mulch on rose beds. Grass clippings rot, mat, and can become an unsightly mess in the rose garden. Put them on the compost heap to decompose, then use the compost in the soil.

*Seaweed* — dried seaweed is a good mulch if properly shredded. Readily available for seashore gardens. Excellent organic material.

*Pine needles* — acid reaction.

*Saw dust* — unsightly. Steals nitrogen from the soil while decomposing.
Some organic mulches have nutritional value, but not in sufficient quantity to influence your choice of a mulch.

## HOW TO APPLY THE MULCH

Before applying mulch, water your rose bed thoroughly to a depth of not less than 10 to 12 inches.
A light mulch such as buckwheat hulls should be applied 1 to 1½ inches deep. Any method of applying is good so long as the mulch is scattered evenly over the entire surface of the bed up to and around

the bush. Do not mound the mulch up into the plant. Rake lightly to remove lumps, moisten, and allow mulch to settle.

## ﹩WHEN TO APPLY THE MULCH

1. Apply the mulch in spring after all winter protection has been removed and all spring chores completed (that is, after the beds have been cleaned, a fungicidal spray applied, the pruning done, and the roses fed their first meal of the season).
2. Mulches have to be renewed from time to time during the summer to maintain their protective depth.
3. Stir the mulch occasionally to keep it from packing.
4. *Winter mulches*, are discussed under Winter Protection. (*See page 132*).

# *Watering*

Water is essential to the life and well-being of the rose because all plant food, whether organic or inorganic (chemical), must be made soluble before it can be taken up by the plant's roots and fed to canes and leaves. To deprive a rose of water, therefore, is to deprive it of food.

Roses not only drink water, they give off incredible amounts of water daily through a process called transpiration. Transpiration means that water in the soil is taken up by the plant's roots, carried through the canes to leaves and petals and there transpired into the air. Experiments show that an average size hybrid tea rose gives off approximately 30 gallons of water in its growing period; established ramblers are believed to transpire as much as 100 gallons a year. This process of transpiration tells us that roses need a constant supply of water maintained in proper balance in the soil throughout the growing and blooming season.

Rainfall in most localities is not sufficient to meet these moisture requirements. To maintain the proper water balance in the soil, we must water the rose beds artificially.

Watering is a pleasant and important chore, so do it yourself, and you will know it has been done thoroughly. Your roses will reward you with vigorous canes, shiny leaves, and beautiful blooms.

Furthermore, I know of no better way to become acquainted with your roses. You'll learn their habit of growth, determine any pruning needs, detect disease or hunger signs, and you may even discover some newly arrived rose pests.

## HOW TO WATER THE ROSE BEDS

1. Water your rose beds at regular intervals throughout the growing and blooming season. In most areas this means *once a week*. If it rains during the week, check the soil to determine how much rainfall has penetrated the mulch and if the moisture reached deep into the bed. It is rare that rainfall does a complete job.

2. Water must soak 8 to 10 inches into the ground to be beneficial to the rose. Watering only the top few inches of the bed is more harmful than helpful, for shallow watering only encourages the growth of a plant's superficial roots and does not reach the big roots that nourish the plant.

3. Water the rose beds early in the morning so the canes and leaves can *dry before noon*. This is important advice, for if moisture remains on leaves and canes longer than six hours, fungus growth is encouraged. The spores of fungus attack only when the plants and soil are moist.

4. Watering should never be done in the late afternoon or evening. The mulch around the bud union remains wet overnight, encouraging crown rot or the spread of crown canker.

5. Never water in the heat of the day. The sun, drying moisture on the leaves, causes leaf-burn.

6. When the weather has been hot, humid, or dry, water-rinse your

bushes early in the morning the day before applying insecticides. Rinsing refreshes the leaves, and often washes away insects.

## SPECIAL WATERING CARE FOR SOILS OF DIFFERENT TEXTURES

1. *Sandy* or *light-textured* soils do not hold moisture. Rose beds of this type may have to be watered two or three times a week in dry climates if the water balance is to be maintained in sufficient quantity to meet the needs of the rose. Nutrients, particularly nitrogen, are leached from light-textured soils by watering and rainfall. Have at least two soil tests done during the summer to determine nutrients needed.

2. If the soil texture is *heavy* or *clayey*, take care not to over-water, for if drainage is inadequate, water pools in the bottom of the bed to create a water-logged condition. Boggy soil deters aeration and therefore deprives roots of much-needed oxygen.

### Watering Miniature Roses

The tiny root system of miniature roses needs constant moisture. Never allow their roots to become dry. However, too much moisture held in heavy, boggy soil is equally bad. Therefore, extra care must be taken when watering these miniature roses.

Miniatures like to have their leaves water-rinsed frequently. Use a fine mist early in the morning, then water their roots.

Don't forget to water your *climbers*, *pillars*, and *shrub roses*. They need water too. These roses are often neglected because they are spread out at various places around the garden.

## WATERING EQUIPMENT

Any of the hose attachments listed and illustrated here are good to use when watering the rose beds.

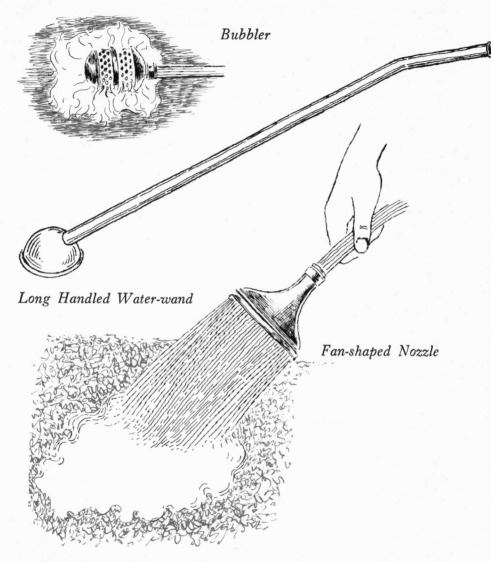

*Bubbler*

*Long  Handled  Water-wand*

*Fan-shaped  Nozzle*

*Long Handled Water-Wand*

The Water-Wand is by far the best attachment. There are several types on the market, but I prefer the one sold by Jackson and Perkins Co., Newark, New York (see their rose catalog).  After the water pressure has been adjusted, you can stand erect, go from bush to bush holding the water-wand close to the mulch, and have no fear of wetting the canes and leaves or splattering them with earth.

### Bubbler

Perforated, ball-shaped nozzle. Good for watering one plant at a time.

### Fan-Shaped Nozzle

Excellent for rinsing foliage or watering the roots. Adjust water pressure; rinse the leaves, don't whip them!

### Plastic Soaker

Plastic soakers come in 50 foot lengths with perforations on one side of the soaker. Place holes downward so that the water can seep into the earth and not spray the leaves. Canvas soakers are good, but unsightly and hard to handle.

### Garden Hose

Use the hose without an attachment. Turn the water pressure low to prevent washing of soil.

### Twin Faucet Connection

Twin connections are time saving. They allow a soaker to work while you use a water-wand.
Cautions:

### Root-Feeders

Do not use root-feeders or water-tubes unless you are a professional, for the water pressure underground loosens the soil and seriously disturbs the root system. One of my friends upheaved two hundred rose bushes by using this method!

### Overhead Water Sprinkler Systems

These can be more harmful than helpful. The amount of water used to irrigate the beds rarely penetrates the mulch or top inch of soil. Leaves, drenched with water, sometimes become sunburned if the sprinklers are used during the heat of the day.

# The Roses' Diet

Roses need a *balanced diet* fed in small amounts at *regular intervals* throughout the growing season and must have a *drink of water* with each meal. Roses, like people, are subject to indigestion when overfed, look puny and have no resistance to disease when undernourished. When a rose plant is in distress, its leaves and blossoms give signals so apparent to the alert rosarian that there seems to be direct communication between plant and gardener.

There are two root systems that feed the rose. The big roots that are planted deep in the soil anchor and nourish the plant, but it is the tiny feeder roots near the surface of the bed that search the soil constantly for food and moisture. See to it that they always have food and water available.

Because soil and climate conditions vary in different parts of the country, it is impossible to give you exact feeding formulas or schedules. For this reason, I urge you to take time, here and now, to understand the basic principles of rose feeding. With such knowledge you can intelligently plan your feeding program and be able to recognize the most common hunger signs. Then, if in doubt about a problem, you can send a few leaves to an agricultural specialist for a diagnosis. Be sure to have a soil test made.

You must also know *when* to feed roses, because roses produce flowers in a recurring cycle of growth, bloom, and rest.

To be specific, the rhythm or cycle begins in early spring with the show of tiny pink leaf-stems. Next comes the development of buds and last, the burst of bloom. As the blooming period wanes, fewer buds appear and the plant goes into a brief, well-deserved rest. It is between these bursts of bloom that a plant's energy is directed to producing new growth. As the new bloom peak approaches, the plant's energies are poured into producing flowers. These cycles recur every four to six weeks until the plant goes into its dormant winter rest.

Roses should not be fed during the waning period. Let them rest; when strong new shoots and buds appear, give them a quick-acting liquid fertilizer or foliar food as a pickup meal. They'll need it to produce the next blooms.

### Sunshine

Sunlight is very important to roses because of a process called photosynthesis. All plant leaves use the indirect energy of the sun to aid in the production of food; the sun's indirect energy joins with carbon dioxide and water to form carbohydrates and thereby liberate oxygen. See to it that your roses have plenty of sun.

## BALANCE THE DIET

The rose's diet is made up of:

        Inorganic Fertilizers (chemicals - minerals)
        Organic Fertilizers (nature's foods)
        Water

These foods may be fed singly or in combination as directed by your soil analysis. Each is essential to the health of the rose, but must be used in correct amounts. *Over-feeding* causes serious problems, and a lack of one or more foods can cause plant anemia (chlorosis). Water must be given with each meal; it is the catalyst that makes these foods available to plant roots in the soil.

## ໄ∾INORGANIC FERTILIZERS (CHEMICALS - MINERALS)

These inorganic elements are quick-acting, readily available foods. Each inorganic element has a specific purpose in the soil, and all are absolutely essential to rose culture.

If the soil lacks any one of the inorganic foods, or if there is an *imbalance* of one or more of these elements, leaves and blooms show definite signs of hidden hunger. (*See Hidden Hunger, p. 105*).

The beginner or amateur rosarian should advise with a garden specialist before applying chemical (inorganic) elements, for many scientists now believe that fewer *inorganic chemical foods* are needed if rose beds are generously supplied with *organic foods* three times a year — early spring, midsummer, and late fall. Many reports show roses to be more vigorous and disease-resistant when given Nature's food, and there is less chance of chemical indigestion.

The three major inorganic elements are:

> Nitrogen
> Phosphorus
> Potassium

### Nitrogen

Nitrogen is the food that stimulates growth. When in balance in the soil, rose canes will be tall and strong, blooms good, and the foliage a rich, dark green.

*An excess of nitrogen* stimulates the plant to produce soft, tall, succulent canes. The plant is thus weakened and has no resistance to summer drought or winter cold. The overuse of nitrogen also encourages the growth of fungus spores.

*The best source of inorganic nitrogen* is Nitrate of Soda.

### Phosphorus

Phosphorus stimulates root growth to produce quality plants and blooms, probably hastens plant maturity and adds winter hardiness. Phosphorus must be incorporated into the lower segment of the rose bed to be of value to the plant roots, for it tends to remain where it is placed in the soil. When used as a top dressing, phosphorus must be cultivated into the top few inches of the rose bed and watered thoroughly to make it available to plant roots.

*The best source of inorganic phosphorus* is Superphosphate 20%.

### Potassium

Potash promotes root growth, but *excessive amounts of potash* deter intake of magnesium and calcium, thereby causing serious problems for the plant. An overdose of potash cannot be corrected.

*A good and safe source of potash* is wood ash from your fireplace. Discuss any potassium deficiency with your garden specialist and be guided by your soil analysis before trying to correct the deficiency.

### ஃ THE MINOR OR TRACE ELEMENTS ARE:

> Calcium, iron, sulphur, boron, iodine, magnesium,
> copper, zinc, manganese, molybdenum.
> Carbon, hydrogen, and oxygen

The term *trace means the amount of minor inorganic elements needed* by a plant; not the amount found in humus, manure, or soil. Calcium, iron, sulphur, boron, iodine, magnesium, copper, zinc, manganese, and molybdenum are obtained from the soil and humus. Carbon, hydrogen, and oxygen are derived from water and from the atmosphere.

Although only small amounts of trace elements are needed in the rose's diet, a lack of one or more may cause serious deficiency diseases; for example, iron deficiency causes chlorosis, a yellow mottling of young leaves, and pale, colorless flowers. This hunger sign is comparable to our developing anemia. (*See Hidden Hunger. p. 105*).

## ORGANIC FERTILIZERS (NATURE'S FOOD)

Organic fertilizers are known as reserve foods, for they release their nutrients in the soil slowly over a period of several weeks.

More and more scientists are writing on the necessity of using nature's organic foods rather than chemicals (inorganic food) for the rose's diet. *Organic nutrients* are slowly released and therefore available to roots over a longer period than chemical fertilizers which are immediately available and readily leached by rainfall or overwatering.

Furthermore, humus and organic foods supply not only the three major foods, nitrogen, phosphorus, and potash, but are the surest way of giving the rose the important trace elements.

If rose beds are prepared with abundant proportions of organic foods, and if these foods are added to the rose bed each year in early spring and midsummer, fewer chemicals will be needed to supplement the diet.

*The organic foods listed below are all commercially available*:

> Bone Meal
> Blood Meal
> Cottonseed Meal
> Fish Meal
> Fish Emulsion (liquid)
> Whale (liquid)
> Cow Manure - composted or dehydrated
> Sheep Manure - composted or dehydrated

To help you plan the rose diet, I have given here a brief outline of the potential of each organic food listed above.

> *Bone Meal* (ground bone)

Approximately 3% Nitrogen, 24% Phosphorus, little or no Potash.

Bone meal, low in nitrogen, is one of the best organic reserve foods. It decomposes slowly over a period of 5 to 6 weeks. Bone meal will not burn plant roots, may be used freely, and can be mixed with other fertilizers. Bone meal may be safely applied at any time of the year, but its nutrients become available in the soil only in warm weather.

*Steamed bone meal* is low in nitrogen, but has a high proportion of phosphoric acid.

*Use*: 1 cup per plant

5 lbs. per 100 square feet

### Blood Meal (dried animal blood)

Approximately 14% Nitrogen, 2% Phosphorus, 1% Potash. Blood meal is one of the best sources of nitrogen and trace elements. Because of its high nitrogen content, it tends to burn roots when used in excessive amounts. A thin sprinkling of blood meal over the surface soil is sufficient to stimulate bacterial growth in the soil.

Blood meal may be used instead of nitrate of soda (inorganic food) to furnish nitrogen when needed.

*Use*: ¼ cup per plant

### Cottonseed Meal

Approximately 7% Nitrogen, 3% Phosphorus, 2% Potash.

Cottonseed meal, an excellent, slow-acting, organic food, tends to encourage luxuriant foliage. May burn roots when used in excessive amounts. Good source of nitrogen. Not as potent as blood meal.

*Use*:   ¼ cup per plant

### Fish Meal

Approximately 10% Nitrogen, 6% Phosphorus, little or no Potash. Fish meal is an excellent reserve food. Derived from sea-going fish. Some fish meal products now available contain chelates to control plant anemia (chlorosis).

*Use*: ¼ cup per plant

### Fish Emulsion (liquid)

5% Nitrogen, 1% Phosphorus, 1% Potash.

Fish Emulsion is derived from sea-going fish and contains all major and minor inorganic elements in highly soluble form. High nitrogen content.

*Mix:* 1 tablespoon to 1 gallon of water
    Pour 1 gallon of mixture around each bush.

### *Whale* (liquid)

Used by some rosarians. Not readily available in most areas.

### *Cow Manure* (well rotted)

Cow manure is not high in nutritive value and can be used in generous amounts. Its primary function is to bring live bacteria (maybe earthworms) to the soil and improve its texture.

Manure should be well rotted (six months old) before being used in or on rose beds.

When preparing beds, incorporate generous quantities of manure into the top 10 to 12 inches of the bed, never deeper if it is to benefit the rose plant, for it is doubtful that bacteria in manure remain active below that level.

### *Dehydrated Manures*

Dehydrated cow or sheep manures may be used as substitutes for natural manure if mixed in careful proportions with compost, leafmold or peat moss. Dehydrated manures are low in nutrients and will not improve soil texture. This product is expensive and in my opinion is a poor substitute.

### *Composted Cow Manure*

Composted cow manure is a new commercial product. Naturally composted manure has no odor and is more effective than dehydrated manure. Apply to surface soil in early spring. Scratch in, water well. Actually, there is no substitute for good, "old-fashioned", well-rotted cow manure, but it is not available in many areas.

### *Sheep Manure — Composted* (commercial product)

A new product — composted sheep manure combined with ground tobacco stems. Excellent food. Apply generously to surface soil in early spring. The tobacco may help to control insect pests.

## FEEDING ESTABLISHED ROSES

### ॐ WHEN, WHAT AND HOW TO FEED

Roses need a varied menu, and prefer small amounts fed often rather than large meals fed once or twice a year.

As you already know, roses require both organic and inorganic fertilizers. Inorganic (chemical-mineral) fertilizers are available at garden supply stores as separate elements, or packaged as complete "Rose Foods."

Before buying any of these commercial products, read the information on each label and note the percentage of nitrogen, phosphorus, and potash present. These elements are represented on the label by numerals, and are always in the same order. Some of the better products now have an organic base and trace elements added.

Study your soil analysis. Then, search for a formula most suited to your roses' needs. Be sure you buy a product devised especially for feeding roses, and do not be persuaded to use a product formulated to feed grass, plants, or shrubs. Feed only as directed on the label.

### ॐ COMPLETE ROSE FOODS ARE AVAILABLE IN THREE FORMS:

1. *Dry* (Powder)
This type of fertilizer is used for root feeding. It must be spread evenly over the surface soil, scratched in, and watered well.
2. *Liquid Foods or Emulsions*
These fertilizers are for root feeding. They must be mixed with water in a pail or sprinkling can and poured or sprayed over the surface soil.
3. *Foliar Foods* (*crystals or liquid*)
These important foods are designed to feed the plant through its *leaves* and contain vitamins and hormones. Foliar foods must be

mixed with water and sprayed or poured over the foliage. The leaf rapidly assimilates the nutrients after application to the foliage, but these nutrients are absorbed only as long as the moisture remains on the leaf. Foliar food products were formulated primarily for leaf feeding, but they are now being used extensively for root feeding as well.

Foliar foods are versatile in their uses. They can be fed at intervals of from two to three weeks and may be added to insecticides. This combination ties in nicely with your insect control program because both can be used at the same time, making it possible to do two jobs in one.

We have quite a choice of foliar foods today. Rapid-Gro was the leader in this field, and, in my opinion, is still the best.

## THE FIRST MEAL IN SPRING SHOULD BE ORGANIC

After the dormant winter period, a rose is hungry and should be fed as soon as the pruning chore is done, the beds cleaned, and before the mulch is applied. This meal should consist of generous amounts of organic matter: bone meal, blood meal, manure (well-rotted or composted). Combine these organic reserve foods in proper proportion and spread evenly over the surface of the rose bed. Carefully cultivate into the first inch or so of soil and water well.

Because organic foods are low in nitrogen, root growth is encouraged, but young canes are not stimulated to develop too rapidly before danger of frost has passed.

## THE SECOND MEAL IN SPRING

This meal is given to stimulate cane and leaf growth. *Root* feed your roses when the new shoots are about two inches long.

Unless otherwise directed by your soil test, feed each plant a complete inorganic rose food formula. These fertilizers are available in dry or liquid form.

Liquid fertilizers and emulsions are to be mixed with water and poured over the surface of the bed. Liquid foods are therefore more readily available to plant roots than dry foods.

Any of the following products are excellent for this second meal.

*Root feed*:

Atlas Fish Emulsion 5-1-1 (in solution)
Contains all major and minor elements in highly soluble form.
Mix: 1 tablespoon to 1 gallon of water and pour 1 gallon of the mix-
    ture around each plant.

Or use a liquid rose food, such as:
Rapid-Gro (Crystals) (23-19-17)

Follow directions on label for *root feeding*, not *leaf feeding*. There are other excellent liquid rose foods available, too many to list here.

If for the second meal you prefer to use a dry, inorganic food formula instead of liquid fertilizers, use any one of the well-known, commercially packaged dry rose foods. There are too many of these products on the market to list.

The usual directions for applying dry fertilizers are:
1 level tablespoonful or 1 handful per plant; scatter over the surface soil around each plant or spread evenly over the entire bed; scratch in and water thoroughly. Rinse leaves to remove any fertilizer when watering the food into the soil, to prevent leaf burn.

ᘺ THE THIRD MEAL

The third feeding is given when the new buds and foliage are fully developed (just before the buds show color). For this meal use a *foliar food*. Foliar feedings may be repeated every two weeks until

September 15, except during the rest cycle (*see The Roses' Diet, p. 72*).
Foliar foods may be combined with insecticides. Be careful when using such combinations in hot, dry spells or in hot, humid periods. A serious phytotoxic condition can develop from the overuse of chemicals in such weather.

Use:  Rapid-Gro (23-19-17)
Mix:  4 level teaspoons to 1 gallon of water.

Or use: Ortho Liquid Rose Food (8-12-4)
Follow directions for foliar feeding as shown on the label.
There are a number of foliar foods on the market, too numerous to list here.

### How to Use Foliar Foods

1. Apply foliar foods with a pressure sprayer or sprinkling can. It is important to saturate both sides of the leaves whenever possible. A pressure sprayer is the best means of applying foliar foods.
2. When mixing liquid rose foods for leaf feeding (foliar feeding), be sure you mix exactly as directed, and *do not use* the directions on the label given for *root feeding*. Such an error could burn up the leaves.
3. Foliar foods should be sprayed over the foliage early in the morning or in the late afternoon, for leaves absorb the food only as long as the moisture remains on the leaf.
4. Never apply foliar foods during hot, dry spells or in very hot, humid weather. If your roses need food at such a time, apply a dry or liquid root food. It is safer than taking the chance of burning the leaves.

### Add iron to the Diet

Native garden soil is often deficient in iron. Yet the deficiency may not be enough to cause such symptoms as chlorosis (*see Hidden Hunger, p. 105*). I recommend using a dose of Sequestrene (iron chelate) as a protective measure twice a season, particularly in New England where iron is usually deficient in native soil. This dose should be given as a foliar food as soon as the leaves are fully developed, approximately June 1, and may be repeated the last week of July. Iron chelate can do no harm and may do a lot of good. Do not spray in hot weather.

*Add Magnesium Too*

When the foliage is fully developed, scatter 1 tablespoon of Epsom Salts over the soil around each plant and water thoroughly.

*Condition Your Plants for Winter*

1.  After August 15 do not root feed nitrogen. Nitrogen fed too late in summer encourages succulent new growth that will not have time to harden before the first frost.
2.  In mid-August sprinkle one handful 0-20-20 (no nitrogen) around each bush to help condition the plants for winter. An additional cup of bone meal per plant at this time can do no harm and may do a lot of good.
3.  Regular foliar feedings may be continued as late as mid-September if your plants appear hungry. The nitrogen in foliar foods is so rapidly assimilated after application that the chance of overstimulating growth is minimized.

## FEEDING NEWLY PLANTED ROSES

If the rose bed was properly prepared and well supplied with organic material and reserve foods before your roses were planted, they will not need inorganic foods in early spring. Wait until their buds are well developed and feed as directed for established roses.

In order to be helpful, I have used trade names of rose foods now available. I hesitated to do this, because products change so rapidly that the beginner is often bewildered at not finding the product mentioned in garden supply stores. Do not let this disturb you. You now have enough information about the organic and inorganic foods to know what to look for and what to buy according to your roses' needs.

# Pruning

Pruning is not an exact science, but can become an art when properly applied, and has concerned the rose lover throughout the ages. Two thousand years ago Pliny the Elder was advising rosarians to "put the torch to your roses each spring so the bush will be burned back to six inches from the ground and thus be forced to send out new wood." He was correct in that pruning does encourage the plant to send out new wood, but rose growers no longer believe in sacrificing any more of a healthy, green cane than is necessary. Furthermore, in our times we have pruning shears with steel blades, chrome-plated handles, and comfort grip with which to do our pruning!

Pruning plays an important part in the health of your roses. It is done primarily to encourage the development of new canes and a maximum of bloom.

To me, pruning is a subject that cannot be taught via lectures or books. It should be demonstrated in a rose garden using live plants and proper pruning equipment. So, if possible, visit the garden of a nearby rosarian and ask for a demonstration.

## ᘛ SPRING PRUNING — WHEN AND HOW

Pruning mature, established hybrid tea roses, grandifloras and flori- bundas begins in early spring when the danger of severe frost is over, while the plant is still dormant, and before the sap begins to "run". This means early March to April first in cold regions of the country, midwinter in warmer climates. Ask a nurseryman in your vicinity when to start pruning.

Plan your pruning program carefully. Do not rush the job, and remember that each bush must be pruned and shaped to its individual needs.

*Save Wood:*

*Save every inch of green wood* possible to produce leaves. Leaves are the rose's food factory. Also, by pruning to save healthy wood, roses will bloom earlier and more profusely in the spring.

*Before making your first cut:*

1. Remove enough soil to expose the crown and bud union.

*Expose Bud Union*

2. Carefully identify all canes that have to be completely cut back to their base; that is:

Old canes that have served their usefulness
Dead canes
Canes injured by "winter-kill"
Diseased canes
Suckers that start below the bud union.

3. Remove all useless *twigs* or small canes that rub or cross each other. The removal of this useless wood will allow light and air to reach the center of your plant when it has completely leafed out.

4. Next, determine how many healthy canes will remain to shape the bush. A healthy rose plant should have developed enough *replacement canes* during the summer to have three to six strong canes re-

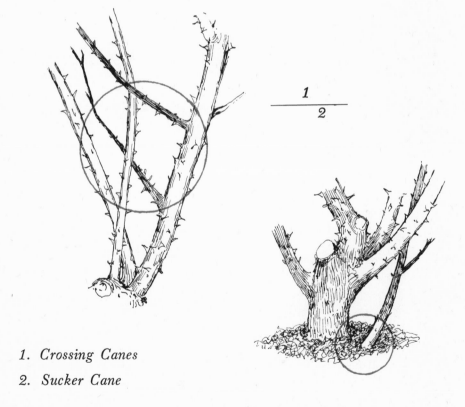

$$\frac{1}{2}$$

1. *Crossing Canes*
2. *Sucker Cane*

maining after pruning. When pruning is completed, the bush should have an open, vase-like shape.

5.  The next step is to determine how much of the remaining healthy canes can be saved. In other words, how much of the brown area ("winter-kill") above healthy, green wood has to be removed.

### Winter-Kill

"Winter-kill" is Mother Nature's way of pruning and describes the brown, injured part of a cane, above healthy green wood. To prune these injured canes, begin cutting *below the brown area*. Continue cutting the cane inch by inch until the pith, or center of the cane, is a healthy, pale yellowish-green. End by cutting above a strong bud eye pointing outward.

If the winter has been severe, several canes may have been killed to their base. If so, do not sacrifice the bush. Cut the dead canes off at their base, and weeks later the plant may surprise you with vigorous new growth — at least give it a try.

In regions where there has been little or no winter-kill, old rose bushes can be cut back 16 to 18 inches from the ground to force the plants to produce new wood and keep the plants symmetrical.

After your plants are in full leaf, if any brown tips (dieback) develop, cut off the brown area to healthy green wood $1/4$ inch above the first strong "eye" on the cane or stem. Removing dead tips will encourage a flower stem to develop below the cut.

Before returning the soil to around the bud union, after the pruning job is over, carefully examine the crown and superficial roots for any growth or disease (*see Canker-Crown-Gall, p. 104-105*).

### Sucker Canes

To identify a sucker cane, pull back the mulch to expose the bud union. Suckers are rank growing canes that start below the bud union from the understock on which the rose was grafted. Leaves on suckers are smaller, differently shaped, and lighter in color than leaves on the main growth. There is a mistaken idea that a seven-leaf leaflet is indicative of suckers. This is incorrect. Many roses develop seven-leaf leaflets from time to time.

If the cane in question starts *from the bud union or above*, it is a much-wanted, new, basal replacement cane. Before cutting any cane at this juncture, make sure you are not mistaking a good basal shoot for a sucker! This has been done many times to the chagrin of amateur rosarians.

*Important Advice*

1. After the pruning job has been completed, saturate the canes and ground with Phaltan (fungicide) or any recommended dormant spray.

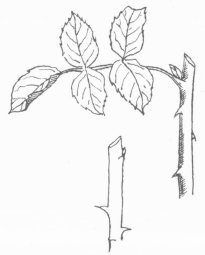

*The Correct Cut*
*¼ inch above a bud eye*

2. You are admonished by all rosarians *never to leave more than ¼ inch of wood above any bud eye.* The bud eye is found on a stem or cane just above the leaf juncture. If the stem or cane at this point is left longer than ¼ inch, the wood above the eye dies back and deters development of a flower stem at this vital point. Furthermore, the dieback that consequently occurs above the cut creates a vulnerable spot for the invasion of parasites (fungus disease) or insects' eggs (larvae).

3. Never use dull pruning shears, knives, or loppers. They tear cane-bark leaving open wounds to invite canker infection, dieback,

and many other problems.  I have seen entire rose gardens destroyed by the use of dull, dirty pruning equipment.

Some rosarians recommend sealing all pruning cuts with shellac, grafting wax or asphalt tree paint.  These materials disfigure the canes and, I find, cause more damage and dieback than does the occasional borer.

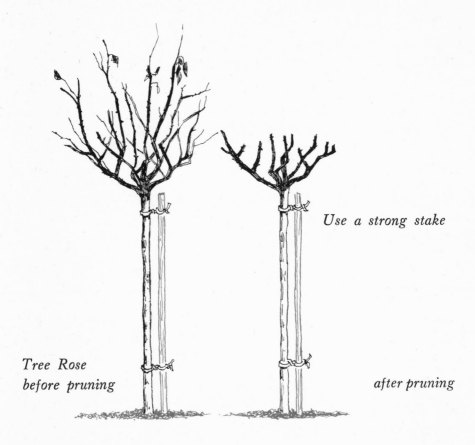

*Use a strong stake*

*Tree Rose*
*before pruning*

*after pruning*

*Pruning Tree Roses*

At spring pruning:
1.  Remove any dead or injured canes.
2.  Cut back remaining canes to 8 or 10 inches from the bud union.

3.  Take out crossing canes or unnecessary twigs.

Tree roses must be hard pruned each spring to maintain their shape. Careful shaping of tree roses continues throughout the growing and blooming season by removal of fading blooms.

### Pruning Climbing Roses or Pillar Roses

1.  In spring remove only dead or injured canes. Major pruning, such as removal of old canes, should be done immediately after the blooming season, in late June or early July.
2.  Large flowering climbers do not produce many new canes a year, so old canes should be removed only after replacement canes are well established.
3.  Cutting off fading blooms ¼ inch above the first leaflet below the flower or cluster will encourage new buds to develop.

Pruning climbing roses is made easy if you plant the variety best suited to your location. Don't try to prune the plant to fit the area. Growth habits must be taken into consideration when planting climbers, for some vigorous climbers develop 30 ft. canes, while others grow to only 8 or 10 feet.

Watch out for suckers. Climbers have them too!

### Pruning Ramblers

Ramblers produce best on one-year-old canes. Prune ramblers immediately after they bloom to allow space for new productive canes. Ramblers develop into an uncontrollable tangle of briars when left unpruned.

### Pruning Shrub Roses

These hardy roses do not need much pruning except to occasionally thin out the canes to keep the plant in shape.

### Pruning Miniature Roses

I prune them exactly as I do their large counterparts, but instead of using pruning shears and loppers, I use my manicure scissors! Prune them to 2 to 3 inches in early spring to maintain their miniature proportions. Some varieties will grow to a foot or more if left unpruned.

Pruning keeps the rose plant healthy, speeds up the blooming cycle, and must be continued throughout the growing season by the removal of:
1. Fading blooms
2. Shoots that develop normally, but do not produce buds.
3. Twigs or crossing canes, to allow light and air to reach the center of the plant
4. Diseased or injured canes that develop dieback.

### Candelabra Canes

New, strong basal canes often develop candelabra-type heads if left to go their own way. Personally, I like them, for these "heads" produce many blooms, although the flowers are usually smaller than those produced on a single cane. I let the buds develop and bloom, remove each flower as it fades, and then when all the buds have opened, I cut the candelabra head back to ¼ inch above the first five-leaflet on the cane. This encourages lateral stems to develop and produce blooms.
To eliminate candelabra heads, you must "rub off" the tip of a new basal cane with your fingers, when the new cane is 12 to 14 inches high. This "rubbing off" of the tip encourages the basal cane to produce lateral flower-stems. Watch to see if the laterals produce buds. If a new lateral is non-productive, cut off its tip back to ¼ inch above the *first* five-leaflet on the stem. A strong flower stem will develop at this point.

### Disbudding

If single blooms are wanted for exhibition or for superior blooms in the garden, side buds on a flower stem must be removed when they have developed sufficiently to determine the rudimentary stem.
Disbud by snapping the tiny bud sidewise with thumb and forefinger, being careful not to disturb the main flower bud. For information on exhibition roses I refer you to the American Rose Society for a list of articles and books on exhibiting roses.

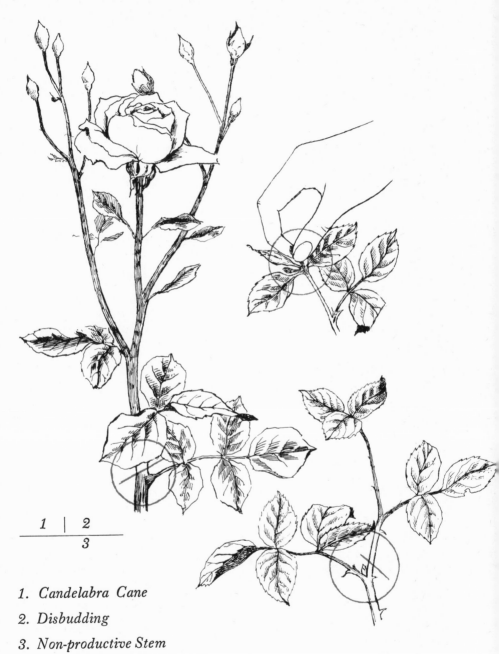

1. *Candelabra Cane*

2. *Disbudding*

3. *Non-productive Stem*

*Cut ¼ inch above a five leaflet to encourage a flower stem to develop at this point*

### Fading Blooms

I believe *fading*, not *faded*, blooms should be removed. By removing fading blooms and not waiting for them to die and drop their petals, you encourage the next blooming cycle and keep your garden tidy. So, whenever you go into your rose garden, take a large paper bag or basket and good sharp shears with you, and keep the fading flowers removed.

To remove fading flowers, cut ¼ inch above the first strong five-leaflet below the fading bloom. This is the point at which a new flower stem will develop. However, to shape the plant, you may have to drop down to the next five-leaflet to have the new stem point outward or inward, as needed to shape the bush. Rarely will a flower stem develop if the cut is made above a three-leaflet.

## FALL PRUNING

Fall pruning is not necessary and can be harmful, for roses use the carbohydrates stored in canes for winter food. Therefore, each inch of healthy wood is vital to winter health. If some bushes are very high, cut back the canes one third. Tie them firmly together to prevent them from being whipped about by winter winds and make your earth mounds high enough to keep the roots from being loosened.

## CUTTING ROSES FOR THE HOUSE

The first year a bush is planted, forego the pleasure of cutting roses with long stems because each stem cut long enough for a vase robs the bush of leaves. Leaves should be treasured as you treasure the blossom; they manufacture the energy that is delivered to the roots as food.

Your restraint will be rewarded by profuse bloom in late summer. This will be the time to cut medium-stemmed flowers for the house, for the plant will be going into its dormant winter rest.

1. Cut the blooms preferably in the *late afternoon;* they will last longer. Never cut roses in strong sunlight or in the heat of day.

2. Plunge the entire stem into hot tap water an inch or so below the bloom. Remove after one hour, then plunge stems into cold tap water.

3. Mash one inch of the stem with a hammer to help the bloom to absorb water.

# The Rose and Its Problems

## DISEASES AND INSECT PESTS

Invasions of insects and diseases are cyclical in their attack on roses. In late May and early June when young leaves and buds develop, aphids, various worms, leaf-cutter bees, sawflies and insects of every type arrive to feast on the tender growth. When the hot, humid days of July and August arrive, mildew, blackspot, and rust appear to disfigure the foliage, and canker to girdle and destroy the canes.

But the greatest pest the rose encounters is the over-anxious gardener, the type that regardless of conditions every seven days attacks rose leaves and blooms with a spray-gun or duster filled with lethal chemicals.

Preventive medicine is important, but roses are often over-protected, and to me the theory of regular protective spraying or dusting with insecticides and fungicides once a week is a way of torturing the foliage.

Leaves heavily coated with sprays or dusts cannot carry out their normal functions, and tender new growth, burned by the combination of sun and chemicals, never develops glossy green leaves capable of manufacturing food for the plant.

If the over-anxious gardener would use a little common sense, fewer chemicals, more food and water, proper pruning, and a good mulch, the rose plant would be strong enough to resist most diseases. When insect pests do arrive and diseases appear, the gardener can spray or dust for the immediate problem.

## A GUIDE TO COMMON DISEASES OF ROSES

Listed and described here are a few common rose problems, where to look for them, and how to control them. If a condition cannot be easily recognized, ask your State Agricultural Agent or a garden specialist in your vicinity for a diagnosis. If these specialists cannot come to see your roses, send the infected leaf, cane, or plant to your State Agricultural Station or State Agricultural College. They will tell you what your problem is.

*Fungus Diseases That Attack the Foliage*:
> Blackspot
> Mildew
> Rust

*Cane and Stem Problems*:
> Canker — "wound" fungi (common canker)
> Borers
> Dieback

*Crown and Root Problems*:
> Crown Gall — "wound" tumor
> Crown Canker

## FUNGUS DISEASES OF ROSES

There are three common rose diseases, Blackspot, Mildew, and Rust, and all are caused by microscopic fungi. These tiny parasites live on the carbohydrates of plant leaves and overwinter on canes and in the ground. Though airborne, they can be brought into the rose garden and be carried from plant to plant by aphids or other insects.

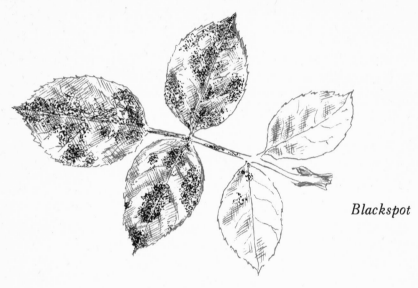

*Blackspot*

### ❧ BLACKSPOT — DIPLOCARPON ROSEA

Blackspot, a devastating and disfiguring fungus disease, attacks rose leaves and will completely defoliate a rose bush if left uncontrolled. This disease cannot be cured — it must be prevented.

Though not prevalent in California nor in arid, desert regions, it is found in varying degrees in all other areas of the United States, Canada, and Europe.

The oft-repeated statement that all roses must have blackspot is a defeatist attitude and is completely unacceptable to me. Blackspot has no place in the private garden. Since it cannot be cured, it must be prevented, for control is a tedious and constant chore.

In my opinion, the only preventive is to dig and burn the plant when the first blackspot-infected leaf appears. I cannot see any reason to fight blackspot year after year on the same bush. It is far less expensive to replace the bush than to spend money buying fungicides to try to control the disease; furthermore, if there is one diseased plant in your garden, it is a constant source of infection for all the other roses.

*Leaf Symptoms*:

Blackspot is easily recognized by the sudden appearance of one or more dark, circular spots on mature lower leaves of the rose bush. These spots rapidly develop fringed edges and often merge into one or more large spots on the leaf. As the fungus disease spreads, the tissue between the black spots turns yellow and the leaf, deprived of cholorphyll, dries and drops. If the infection is allowed to spread to a large portion of the foliage, defoliation will weaken the plant with subsequent loss of the bush. (*See plate, p. 96*).

*Controls* — From the moment blackspot is detected:

1. Saturate *all plants* in the rose bed and the surface soil with a fungicidal spray or dust. Spraying is preferable to dusting.
2. Remove *every infected leaf* from the bush and all leaves, or bits of stems, from the ground because leaves or wood infected with fungus spore of blackspot, if left to rot in or on the ground, remain a potential source of reinfection year after year. (Burn all debris.)
3. Change the mulch and top soil or turn it under to bury any portion of an infected leaf or cane that might remain on the surface soil.

*Some recommended fungicides*:

*Phaltan* (Folpet)

Mix: 1 level tablespoon of 75% wettable powder to 1 gallon of water. Phaltan leaves a white residue on the foliage, but at present seems to be as near a specific for blackspot as any fungicide on the market.

or

*Captan* (*Orthocide contains 50% Captan*)

Mix and use: As directed on package.
Whenever possible, apply the fungicide *before* a predicted rain to

put a protective film on the leaves. The fungicide must remain on the foliage three days to be effective. If a rain washes the leaves during this period, spray or dust as soon as possible after the leaves dry.

MILDEW — (SPHAEROLTECA PANNOSO ROSEA)

*Rose mildew*, a common rose disease, is disfiguring, but is not as serious a disease as blackspot. Some varieties of roses are far more susceptible to mildew than others.

*Leaf Symptoms*:

Mildew *appears in early spring* and can be identified by a white, powdery coating on tender new growth and young buds. At this

*Mildew*

beginning stage the infection can be controlled, even cured, but if left to progress, young buds rarely develop, leaves crinkle and die, and the fungus spreads rapidly to cover and destroy older leaves and stems.

Mildew develops when hot, humid summer days are followed by cool nights. These fungus spores are most active when the thermometer registers between 65° and 75° F.

Poor air circulation (micro-climate) and dry roots are conducive to the development of the disease.

See to it that your roses have a balanced diet. The overuse of nitrogen is bad because mildew spores prefer succulent new growth.

*Controls:*

*Mildew can be controlled*, and possibly cured, if when it first appears, you apply any one of the following:

*Acti-dione PM* (antibiotic) is now used extensively for the eradication of mildew, but should be used carefully and exactly as directed on the package or you may injure the plant. Applying at 10 to 14 day intervals is usually adequate to control the problem.

Acti-dione PM can be added to insecticides or foliar foods.

*Phaltan* (Folpet) — fungicide

Mix: 1 level tablespoon of 75% wettable powder to 1 gallon of water. Repeat once a week until mildew is controlled.

> or

*Captan* (Orthocide contains 50% Captan)

Mix and use:  As directed on package.

> or

*Karathane* — an efficient fungicide for control of powdery mildew.

Difficult to obtain.

Mix: ½ teaspoon to 1 gallon of water.

Caution:

In hot weather reduce any fungicidal spray or dust formula to one-half the recommended strength and apply every 3 or 4 days instead of every 7 to 10 days. This procedure is safer than using strong dosages at longer intervals.

*Bicarbonate of Soda* — Mix: 1 tablespoon to 1 gallon of water. A stronger solution may be used if necessary.
Bicarbonate of Soda Solution is one of the simplest controls of mildew. I have used it with great success for mildew on my miniature roses. It may discolor full-blown blooms, but it does not affect buds. The dosage can be increased if deemed necessary.

*Water-Rinsing*: Water-rinsing the foliage in early morning on a sunny day may minimize the spread of mildew.

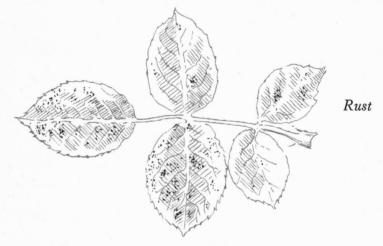

*Rust*

RUST — (PRAYMIDIUM MUCRONATUM)

Leaf rust, common to roses, is more serious on the West Coast than in other regions of the country.
The amateur rosarian should be on the lookout for rust. It develops rapidly, repeats its summer cycle of germination every ten days to two weeks, and takes only four hours of constant moisture on the leaf to develop.

*Leaf Symptoms*:

Rust can be identified by tiny, bright orange-colored spots on the *underside of leaves.* Viewed from the *leaf surface* the spots are light yellow, cup-like depressions.

If uncontrolled, the summer stage of rust develops into orange-red masses of spores on the underside of leaves, causing the surface spots to appear as dead tissue. The spore masses develop so rapidly, the leaf wilts and dies in four to five days.

In late autumn, *black rust* appears. These black spores remain on the plants all winter to start a new growth cycle in the spring.

   *Control:*

*Phaltan* (Folpet) — fungicide

Mix: 1 level tablespoon of 75% wettable powder to 1 gallon of water.

*Cane Canker*

## CANE AND STEM PROBLEMS

### ✿CANKER — "WOUND" FUNGI

Canker, a devastating plant problem, is caused by various types of fungi or parasites entering wounds on a cane or any woody area of the rose plant. There are many types of canker, but we are concerned here with so-called *common* or *stem canker.*

   *Wounds are created by:*

1. Dull pruning shears that leave ragged cuts, and by careless cultivation of the rose bed, injuring canes.
2. Canes that cross or rub, thorns puncturing or tearing the bark.

3. Fading blooms torn off the stem instead of being properly cut off.
4. Tearing off sick leaflets that leave split bark.
5. Frost cracks.

Canker is first noticed as a dark spot on a cane or stem or at the bud union. As this spot enlarges, the bark splits, cracks, and develops corky, calloused ridges, and the area turns a dark brown. If not diagnosed in its early stages, the cankered wound girdles the cane and cuts off the food and water supply above the lesion, with consequent dieback above the strangled area.

*Nursery-infected stock* is the source of most canker, it having been started by careless grafting at the nursery. Carefully inspect all plants before putting them into the rose bed. If you are suspicious of any discoloration or unhealthy bark on a cane or the bud union, have an expert see the cane and diagnose the problem. If the lesion turns out to be canker of any kind, return the plant to the nursery with a loud protest.

One canker-infected plant can devastate an entire rose garden. Therefore, my best advice is promptly to remove the infected plant and replace the soil in the bed in that area. Then saturate all your remaining plants and the ground with a fungicidal spray.

If a fungicide is needed during the hot days of summer, use:

*Phaltan (Folpet)* fungicide

Mix: 1 level tablespoon of 75% wettable powder to 1 gallon of water.

In early spring before the leaf buds break, you can try to control the spread of canker by saturating the surface soil and canes with a dormant spray by using:

*Lime-Sulphur*

Mix: 1 part lime-sulphur to 9 parts water. (It will stain walls.)

*Acme Bordeaux Mixture (dormant spray)* — combination of copper-sulphate and lime-sulphur.
Mix and use only as directed on package.

*How to Control the Spread of Wound Canker*

Using clean, sharp shears, knife, or loppers:

1.  Cut off injured or infected cane back to healthy green wood and remove any dead cane to its base.

2.  Never water rose beds at night.

3.  Saturate infected plant and surface soil with a recommended fungicide.

*Borers — pith or cane injury*

Identified by a hole in the pith of a cane or stem. Bees, sawflies, and beetles deposit their larvae in open wounds, causing dieback. (*See Insect Pests, p. 115*).

*Control:*

1.  When injury first appears, cut cane back to healthy green wood below the borer. Burn dead wood.

2.  Continue using regular insecticide program.

*Dieback*

&❧DIEBACK

There are many causes, and dieback indicates what it says. The tip of a branch becomes progressively sick, dies back to a leaf bud, larger stem, or even to the ground. Dieback can be started by stems that are left too long above a pruning cut, by open cuts left unsealed that invite borers to enter, by canker-infected wounds, or by winterkill.

*Control*:

Prune back dead portion of the cane or stem to healthy green wood above a strong leaf-bud.

*Crown Gall*

## CROWN AND ROOT PROBLEMS

### ꝭ⟶CROWN GALL — ROUNDED TUMOR OR WOUND DISEASE

Dying plants are often indicative of crown gall disease. Large crown gall tumors will be found near the crown and sometimes small tumors on the roots. Crown gall bacteria lives in the soil and can be a source of reinfection for as long as two years. Left undiagnosed these tumors are found when the dead plant is removed from the bed. When a diseased plant is removed, replace all soil in the bed at that area with new soil before replanting. Keep the disease out of the garden by checking plants when you buy them, and by exposing and inspecting the crown at spring pruning.

## CROWN CANKER

Appears as a black water-soaked area at or above the bud union. This type of canker splits the bark and spreads rapidly to canes or roots. It is most destructive in late fall and early spring. Watering at night encourages the spread of crown canker.

*Controls*

Remove diseased plant (burn) and replace soil. Saturate surface soil with a recommended fungicide.

# HIDDEN HUNGER
*Leaf Symptoms*

## CHLOROSIS

We have already learned that good foliage is essential to plant health and that the rose must have a balanced diet. Whenever any of the major or minor inorganic elements are deficient in soil the plant shows the problem by yellowing or yellow and green mottling of leaves. This dramatic leaf symptom is called chlorosis and indicates plant anemia; in other words, the loss of chlorophyll (green coloring matter). Leaf chlorophyll combines with the indirect rays of the sun (photosynthesis) for the production of rose food. So, unless the condition causing chlorosis is recognized and corrected, the starving leaves fall, and the defoliated bush dies of malnutrition.

All deficiency leaf symptoms are more or less alike, so it is difficult to differentiate between the causes. When you are in doubt, ask for professional help, for spray injury creates similar leaf symptoms. Chlorosis caused by spray injury, however, is temporary, while a true element deficiency in the soil is permanent and unless corrected, becomes progressively worse.

᠘᠊᠊ SOME COMMON CAUSES OF CHLOROSIS:

> Iron deficiency
> Magnesium deficiency
> Calcium deficiency
> Nitrogen deficiency
> Oxygen deficiency (poor drainage)
> Insect invasions
> Drought conditions
> Insufficient sunlight

*Iron Deficiency*

1. *Iron Deficiency*

Iron, a trace element, is necessary for the production of chlorophyll (green coloring matter) and is therefore a most important nutrient if our rose bushes are to be covered with beautiful dark green foliage. Iron deficiency can occur in any type soil (loam, sandy, or clay, whether acid or alkaline).

*Iron Chlorosis* — (lime-induced).

This type chlorosis is common in areas where the native soil is highly alkaline or the rose beds have been carelessly overlimed, the reason being that iron is rendered unavailable to plant roots by being "locked" in alkaline soils.

*Leaf Symptoms*:

Young leaves turn yellow while the veins and mid-rib remain green, or the leaves may develop yellow and green mottling. Mature leaves show these symptoms only under extreme conditions.

*To Correct*:

Adjust the pH of the soil if overalkaline. Then, use Sequesterene (iron chelate), a readily soluble powder that can be used for foliar feeding or be applied to the surface soil and watered in to feed the roots. This is by far the best product to use to correct iron deficiency of native soil or lime-induced deficiency.

Sequestrene (iron chelate) may be used in spring and again in mid-summer. This assures beautiful dark green foliage, and certainly can do no harm. I have used it with great success.

*To foliar feed using iron chelate —*

Mix: 1 teaspoon to 1 gallon of water, or 2 tablespoons to 6 gallons of water.

Apply a mist spray to the underside and tops of leaves. Water the surface soil thoroughly following each application to get the benefit of the solution that falls on the mulch.

*To root feed using iron chelate —*

Use: 2 teaspoons scattered around each plant and water in, or use in solution: 2 tablespoons to 1 gallon of water.

Pour 2½ pints of the solution around the average size plant — more for large climbers or shrub roses.

If you cannot obtain Sequestrene (iron chelate).

Use: Iron Sulfate (powder).

Apply 1 teaspoon (dry) around each plant; water in.

*As a foliar spray —*

Mix: 1 ounce of iron sulphate to 3 gallons of water.

2. *Magnesium Deficiency*

So much is said about iron deficiencies that magnesium deficiency is often forgotten. I want to emphasize here that an adequate supply of magnesium is essential to the health of the leaf; therefore, the health of the plant is dependent upon the soil being properly supplied with this trace element.

Magnesium is usually deficient in soils that need periodic liming and in sandy, light-textured soils where nutrients are easily leached by rainfall or overwatering.

*Symptoms*:

The center of mature leaves become pale yellow, and areas of dead tissue develop near the mid-rib.

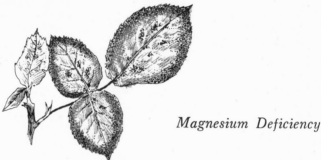

*Magnesium Deficiency*

*To Correct*:

Raise the pH from acid to slightly alkaline.

Apply a dressing of *dolomitic limestone*: 8 ounces per square yard. This application should meet the magnesium requirement of the soil for two years. However, the benefit of the treatment may not be apparent until the second year after application. Dolomitic limestone is effective only if there is adequate rainfall or watering.

*Epsom Salts* (used as a foliar spray for magnesium deficiency). Mix: 2 tablespoons to 2½ gallons of water.

4 ounces to 10 gallons of water.

*When used in dry form,*

Apply ¾ ounce of Epsom Salts per square yard of surface area once a year.

Caution: Epsom Salts must not be mixed with insecticides or fungicides, and care must be taken not to exceed the recommended rates of application.

### 3. *Calcium Deficiency*

Acid soils with a pH of 5 or below are often lacking in calcium.

*Symptoms*:

Leaves turn greenish yellow, edges of leaflets wither, and brown patches appear between leaf margin and mid-rib. Leaves lacking in calcium fall before they are entirely dead; petals become crinkled, and flowers are deformed.

*To Correct*:

Have a soil test made and apply: 2 tablespoons of *lime-calcium* around each plant.

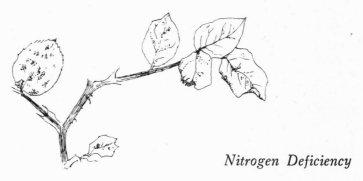

*Nitrogen Deficiency*

### 4. *Nitrogen Deficiency*

This chlorosis symptom is common where nitrogen is readily leached from light-textured, sandy soil by excessive rainfall or watering. However, nitrogen deficiency may also appear when nitrogen is in the soil, but is rendered unavailable to roots due to waterlogged soil conditions.

*Symptoms*:

Nitrogen chlorosis appears first on older foliage. Leaves will be small, pale in color, with tinges of red and yellow. Red spots always accompany nitrogen deficiency, and there is no yellow and green mottling. Plants appear sick, blooms are small, buds fail to develop.

*To Correct*:

Check drainage and correct if necessary.

Improve soil texture by adding peat and humus to rose beds to control leaching.

Feed each plant one or a combination of the following organic foods, high in nitrogen:

Blood Meal — 1 heaping tablespoon

Fish Meal - ¼ cup

Fish Emulsion (liquid) — mix 1 tablespoon to 1 gallon of water and pour 1 gallon of mixture around each plant.

*Nitrate of Soda* (inorganic) —

Nitrate of Soda contains 15% nitrogen and is the most quickly available form of nitrogen. Nitrate of Soda is almost immediately available to plants upon application.

If applied in dry form, moisten soil, then scatter over surface soil: 1 pound to 100 square feet.

If applied in solution:

Dissolve 1 ounce to 2 gallons of water.

My best advice when trying to correct a major inorganic element deficiency is to discuss your soil analysis with a garden specialist, for, I repeat, an overdose of any major inorganic element can be as bad for the rose as the deficiency you are trying to correct.

5. *Oxygen Deficiency*

This leaf symptom indicates insufficient oxygen reaching roots. Poor aeration is caused by bad drainage, waterlogged soil, overwatering, or excessive rainfall.

*Symptoms*:

Leaf veins and mid-rib turn yellow first, then leaf tissue pales, and leaves fall. Leaves become clear yellow.

*To Correct*:

Check and correct any drainage problem.

Add peat and humus until soil is friable (porous) enough to allow oxygen to reach the roots readily.

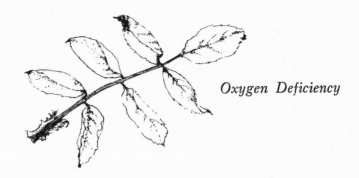

*Oxygen Deficiency*

6. *Insect Invasions* (chlorosis)

Insects cause a mild form of chlorosis by puncturing leaves and sucking the chlorophyll.

*Symptoms*:

Leaves turn yellow, appear dry or scorched, and then fall as if they
had a chemical injury.

*To Correct*:

Saturate both sides of leaves with any good insecticide or miticide,
spray or dust.

7. *Drought Conditions* (chlorosis)

If yellowing or mottling appears in the center or lower segment of
the bush, it may indicate dry roots from drought or lack of watering.
These mottled yellow leaves dry and fall and can defoliate the bush.

*To Correct*:

Water thoroughly at regular intervals until the leaves appear green
and turgid. Check the mulch and humus content of the soil to see
if moisture is being held in proper balance.

Drought conditions can also cause buds to be abnormally small.

### 8. *Insufficient Sunlight*

Chlorosis can be caused by insufficient sunlight.

*To Correct*:

Remove adjacent trees, or move the rose bed!

Don't worry if the blossoms seem to be off-color the first year. This can be expected. New plants cannot develop sufficient root structure during the first months after being planted to adequately nourish the bush and produce true-colored flowers. Soil, rainy seasons, and dry spells also affect the color.

### ᘓ᠊MORE LEAF PROBLEMS — PHOSPHORUS AND POTASH DEFICIENCIES

These leaf symptoms *differ* from those of chlorosis. Leaves become discolored (some appear scorched). These deficiencies can be confused with chemical injury.

### 1. *Phosphorus Deficiency*

This problem is rare in rose beds where a good feeding schedule is maintained.

*Symptoms*:

Leaves develop a grey-green cast, and a purplish tinge on the underside of mature foliage.
Do not confuse these purplish discolorations with the red to purple color of *new growth*. I have a friend who cut off all last year's second growth, believing the plant was sick!

*To Correct*:

According to your soil analysis,
Use:  Superphosphate 20%
1 heaping tablespoon (dry) around each plant.
Remember, phosphorus tends to remain where it is placed in the soil, so when applied to the surface, scratch it in and water thoroughly.

## 2.  *Potassium (Potash) Deficiency*

This deficiency is rarely found in well-prepared beds that are fed generous amounts of organic foods.

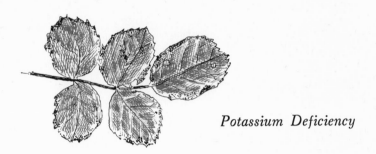

*Potassium Deficiency*

*Symptoms*:

Brown patches develop along leaf margins to eventually form a continuous brown rim of dead tissue resembling leaf scorch. Brown areas also develop between the leaf veins. Chemical burn may cause similar leaf symptoms.

*To Correct*:

A light sprinkling of wood ash from your fireplace is a good source of potash plus calcium. You can also use sulphate of potash applied one-half pound per hundred square feet of ground area. When applying potash, *be careful*, for there is no way to correct an overdose. Let your soil test guide you, and consult with a garden specialist before applying potash.

### VIRUS INFECTION

A common ailment that is not serious in this country, and there is no known cure. Virus infection is transmitted by budding and grafting infected budwood and understock. Research is being done on this problem. Rosarians are beginning to believe that antibiotics are a means of control.

*Mosaic Virus*

*Symptoms:*

Virus symptoms are best seen in mature leaves. They rarely appear on young leaves. The green and yellow zigzag stripes or mosaic patterns are often confused with chlorosis.

## PURPLE SPOTTING

A physiological disorder rather than a disease. This leaf symptom indicates malnutrition accentuated by improper drainage. Do not confuse these dark discolorations with blackspot. Similar small purple spots are sometimes caused by spring frost on immature leaves. If you cannot diagnose the problem, send a few leaves to your agricultural station. Have a soil analysis made at the same time. Correct any drainage problem.

*All corrective advice* given in this book is basic. No book could answer all questions without confusing the amateur. Furthermore, in these busy days no one can spend endless hours searching pages to find the perfect formula or cure for a dozen problems. Many a rose garden has been turned into an experimental station because of an overanxious amateur fearing the bushes have every deficiency and disease. Don't be ashamed to ask for help from a specialist in your vicinity. If you could figure out the cure-alls alone, you'd be the rose specialist.

## INSECT PESTS
### *Leaf Symptoms and Controls*

There are two types of insects that feed on the tissue of rose leaves and blooms — sucking insects and chewing insects. Some of these hop from plant to plant, some fly; there are little green grubs that roll themselves into a leaf, while others deposit their larvae in open wounds on canes and stems to cause dieback.

*Sucking Insects* pierce leaves or stems to suck juices and must be controlled by chemicals that burn or paralyze.

*Chewing Insects* eat leaf tissue and flower petals and are controlled by the use of stomach poisons.

The arrival of these insects is usually cyclical, and they rapidly devellop into large colonies, unless controlled. Weather influences their appearance; some insects prefer hot, dry days and old leaves, while others come in early spring to colonize and enjoy tender young growth.

Science has provided rosarians with specific chemicals to discourage invasions of these insect pests and to kill them and is continually developing better, more specific controls for all rose problems. It is imperative that you know how to identify the most common insects that invade the rose garden and be able to recognize the damage they do to leaves and canes.

Start your spraying or dusting program in the spring as soon as the leaves are well developed. Continue applications of preventive controls every two or three weeks, or as needed, until the plants lose their leaves in the fall, or after the first frost. Certain conditions may impose more frequent applications of specific controls.

Described below are the enemies that keep us constantly on the alert from early spring until late fall, trying to outsmart them. You will also find descriptions of leaf signals that warn us of their arrival, and the names of some insecticides.

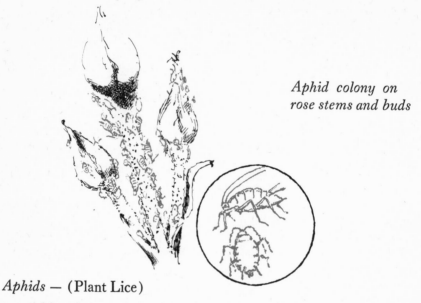

*Aphid colony on rose stems and buds*

*Aphids* — (Plant Lice)

These sucking insects arrive early in spring and are found clustered in colonies on tender foliage and young buds. Unless controlled, the bud will never develop.

Aphids are soft-bodied, pale green, or pink insects. They multiply rapidly, transmit bacteria and fungus spores from one plant to another, and leave a sticky honey-dew on the foliage that attracts bees, flies, and ants.

Aphid colonies are difficult to destroy and may have to be sprayed at three-day intervals until controlled.

*To Control*, use:

Malathion 50% emulsion or 50% wettable powder.
Mix: 1½ teaspoons to 1 gallon of water.
In hot weather it is safer to use Malathion 50% wettable powder in place of emulsion. (Do not combine Malathion with Black Leaf 40).

Or you can use:

Isotox Garden Spray (insecticide-miticide) — contains Malathion 10%, Tedion (miticide), Lindane, D.D.T.

Mix: 1 tablespoon to 1 gallon of water

Or use:

Black Leaf 40 (nicotine sulphate)

Mix: 1½ teaspoons to 1 gallon of water, plus 1 teaspoon soap powder or flakes as a spreader (not a detergent).

Use with care in hot weather — reduce formula.

*Borers* — larvae of bees, sawflies, beetles, etc.

These insects pierce the bark or enter a cane through pruning cuts left unsealed, to deposit their larvae. Borer damage is identified by a small hole in the pith of a cane and by dieback.

*To Control*:

Cut off dead area back to healthy green pith. Burn the dead wood.

*Carpenter Bees* (pith borers) — make nests in pith of rose canes, causing the cane to wilt. Remove wilted or brown area of cane back to healthy wood, and burn infected tip.

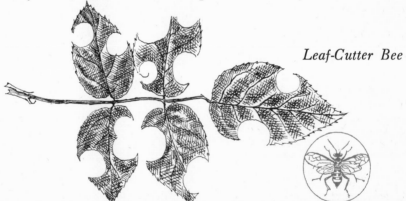

*Leaf-Cutter Bee*

*Leaf-cutter Bees* — chewing insects that cut ovals or circles from leaf margins. These bees chew, but do not eat tissue. The leaf-cutter bee uses chewed material to line its nest. There is practically no way to control the leaf-cutter bee because this insect does not use the chewed material as food. A stomach poison, then, is of little value.

*Japanese Beetles* —(chewing insects)
The mature beetle is difficult to kill. If chemicals are strong enough to destroy the beetle, they will also seriously injure the rose leaves and flowers. The best thing to do is to fill a jar or pail with some detergent or kerosene, hand pick the devils and put them in the container.

*To control the grubs that live in the lawn*: Spray the ground with Chlordane. Consult your garden specialist on what to use on your lawn to kill the Japanese beetle grub.

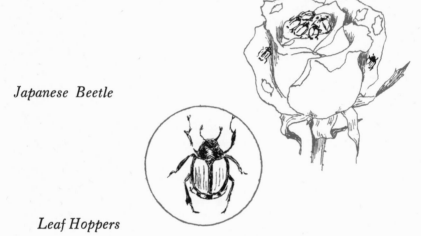

*Japanese Beetle*

*Leaf Hoppers*

These sucking insects lay eggs beneath leaf cuticle; nymphs emerge to suck the juices; mottled designs appear on the surface of leaves. Disturb the bush, and you will find leaf-hoppers jumping about in the foliage.

*To Control*:

Black Leaf 40 (nicotine sulphate) — an old but excellent product.
Mix: 1½ teaspoons to 1 gallon of water plus 1 teaspoon soap powder or flakes as a spreader (not a detergent).
Use with care in hot weather — reduce formula.
A systemic applied to roots or leaves may prove effective as a control of leaf hoppers.

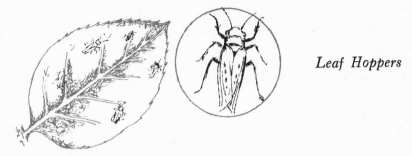

*Leaf Hoppers*

### *Leaf-Rollers* — (Caterpillars)

Green caterpillars curl themselves into a leaf and seal the edges while they feed on leaf tissue. Cut off the leaf and burn. Leaf-rollers are practically impossible to kill by spraying or dusting.

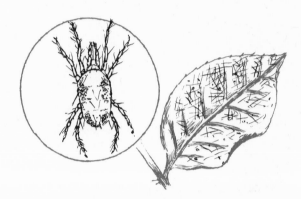

*Red Spider Mites*

### *Mites — Red Spider*

These microscopic sucking insects arrive in hot, dry weather and multiply rapidly. They pierce undersides of leaves, suck leaf juices, and hide under a cobweb-like cover. Leaves infested with spidermites appear dry and yellow, and then fall.

An infestation of red spider is a serious problem for the rose, so be on the constant look-out in dry, hot weather for this devastating mite. Be suspicious of parched leaves. To find the mites, place a piece of white paper under the leaf and gently tap the leaf with a pencil. The little red mites will fall on the paper, and you will see them scurrying about.

*To Control*:

Use any good miticide, such as:

*Kelthane* 18% liquid emulsion or 18% wettable powder (do not combine Kelthane with Isotox or Malathion).
Mix:   2 teaspoons to 1 gallon of water.

Aramite 15% wettable powder.
Mix:   1 tablespoon to 1 gallon of water.

Black Leaf 40 (nicotine sulphate) — an old product, but still one of the best for control of spidermites.
Mix:   1½ teaspoons to 1 gallon of water, plus 1 teaspoon soap powder or flakes as a spreader (not a detergent).

Tedion
Mix:   1 tablespoon to 1 gallon of water.
Repeat the control in one week, if necessary.

Water rinsing the foliage during hot, dry weather often gives good protection against mites if done thoroughly every four or five days.

*Rose Budworms*

The larvae of the bordered sallow moth roll themselves into tender foliage, seal the leaf they are in and the leaves around them with a sticky web, and eat holes into the tender adjoining bud.

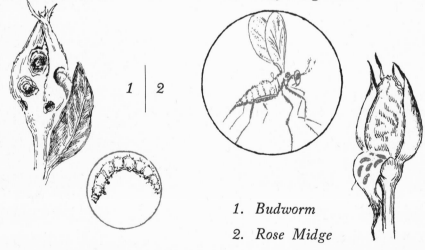

1 | 2

1.  *Budworm*
2.  *Rose  Midge*

These caterpillars, a half inch long or longer, are greenish with longitudinal dark stripes and black markings, or with orange marks.

*To Control*:

Cut off bud and leaves to a strong bud-eye. Crush worm and burn debris.

### Rose Midge

These microscopic insects attack flower buds, leaf buds, and tips of new shoots, giving them a scorched or blackened appearance. Snip off and burn injured leaf or bud.

*To Control*:

Use Methoxochlor 15% wettable powder.
Mix:   2 teaspoons to 1 gallon of water
             or
Use an all-purpose spray containing Methoxochlor. Methoxochlor is less toxic to humans and animals than D.D.T. and is a good substitute. Spray ground and plants. Two applications given seven days apart may be necessary to control midge.

### Sawflies — (Rose Slugs)

These insects eat leaf tissue between veins, leaving foliage skeletonized.

*Rose Slug*

*To Control*:

Spray or dust the foliage with:
D.D.T. 50% wettable powder.

Mix:   2 tablespoons to 1 gallon of water

*To Control*, use:

Malathion 50% emulsion or 50% wettable powder
Mix 1½ teaspoons to 1 gallon of water
> or

Methoxochlor 15% wettable powder
Mix:  2 teaspoons to 1 gallon of water.

*White Flies* — (sucking insects).

It is the nymphs of white flies that cause the damage. They cluster on the undersides of leaves, suck juices, and excrete honeydew which causes a sooty mold on the leaf. Leaves become dry and yellow, and fall. Defoliation of the bush will occur if white flies are not controlled.

When a bush is agitated and miniature white moths fly about, it means the damage has been done — but spray at once. Watch for signs of white flies in hot, dry weather.

*To Control*, use:

Malathion 50% emulsion or 50% wettable powder.
Mix:  1½ teaspoons to 1 gallon of water
> or

Black Leaf 40 (nicotine sulphate).
Mix: 1½ teaspoons to 1 gallon of water, plus 1 teaspoon soap powder or flakes as a spreader (not a detergent).

Black Leaf 40 can be combined with Isotox Garden Spray (no soap powder or flakes needed). Do not combine Black Leaf 40 with Malathion.

*Thrips*

These are small, slender insects with two pairs of narrow wings. They live on petals and buds, and hide deep in the heart of the rose. Pull back the petals, and you will find them scurrying to a better hiding place. They prefer yellow or light colored blooms.

If the edges of the flower petals appear scorched and discolored, and fully developed buds show color, but do not open, be on the alert. Thrips appear in early summer and are practically impossible to kill. Cut off any infected bloom or bud to the next leaf bud and burn the infected bloom.

If thrip invasion is serious, my best advice is to cut all buds that show color and burn. This is the only procedure that I know of which will control thrips in my area.

Covering the buds every few days with D.D.T. or Malathion may help, but I doubt it. Furthermore, you may burn the foliage while trying to control the thrips.

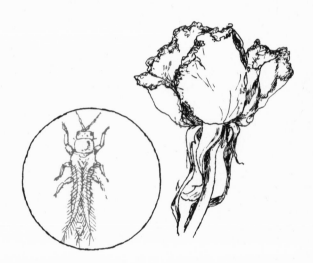

*Thrips*

## SPRAYING OR DUSTING IS SERIOUS BUSINESS

Control of insect pests is a meticulous job, but not a difficult one. It takes patience and understanding of the problem; so whenever possible, do the spraying or dusting yourself. Gardeners, no matter how good, may not be as infatuated with the roses as you are and may take this duty as a chore instead of a pleasure. The time of day to apply chemicals is also important, and the gardener, pressed by many duties, will spray or dust at his convenience, not at the time best suited to the rose.

There are many and varied commercially packaged products that combine insecticides, fungicides, and miticides. These products are formulated to allow the gardener to do several jobs in one and are available for either spraying or dusting.

All-purpose products are excellent, but there are times when the use of a specific chemical is more effective. Some commercial products are formulated to combat *insect pests only*, while others incorporate fungicides for the *control of fungus diseases*. It is therefore very important when buying separate chemicals or all-purpose sprays and dusts that you read carefully the recommended use of each product before buying. Let me caution you not to mix chemicals unless you are so directed by a garden specialist, for many garden chemicals used for garden sprays or dusts are incompatible.

### Chemicals Can Cause Problems (Allergies)

Some gardeners are allergic to certain chemicals. If you fit into this category, you may find it necessary to experiment until you discover insecticides or fungicides that agree with you and disagree with the pests!

### Phytotoxicity — the plant has its problems too.

When an excess of insecticides or fungicides is applied to the foliage, the plant, because of an overdose of chemicals, develops within its system a toxic condition known as phytotoxicity. The plant subsequently dies of chemical poisoning. Phytotoxicity can be influenced by weather conditions (humidity and temperature) and by the use of chemicals that are incompatible.

### Tree Sprays

When your roses are in leaf, protect them from chemicals used while shade or fruit trees adjacent to the garden are being sprayed. Water your roses before spraying starts and rinse them well after the job has been completed. Tree chemicals will burn and often kill the rose leaves.

## SPRAYING VS. DUSTING

Some rosarians recommend dusting, because it is easy to apply, but sprays are easy to mix and are more effective for many problems.

*When using insecticides, fungicides, or miticides*, read the directions carefully and *do not increase amounts* given. Spray early in the morning or in the late afternoon.

1. When spraying, mix chemicals as directed with water and *use at once*. Do not save mixture for use at a later time.

2. Agitate the container often while spraying.

3. Cover surface of all leaves with chemical. Then, *thoroughly* coat the *underside* of the leaves — this is where most insect colonies and diseases originate.

4. When using a pressure sprayer, stand 3 to 4 feet away from the bush, allowing only the mist to reach the foliage. The heavy force of the spray can cause leaf-burn.

5. Never spray on a hot, humid day or when the temperature is 80° or above; chemicals on such days are apt to burn the foliage and disfigure the bush for the rest of the blooming season.

6. In midsummer during hot, humid, or dry weather, cut the amount called for on the package by one-fourth to avoid leaf-burn.

7. Try to apply fungicides before a rain to discourage the growth of fungus spores.

8. *Wash all spray apparatus* well when job is finished.

9. *Have special sprayers for use in the rose garden only.* Never use a sprayer that has been used to apply chemicals to trees or weeds — you may seriously injure your rose plants.

10. After spraying or dusting, wash all exposed skin areas. Keep children and pets in the house until the spray or dust job is completed.

11. *When dusting*, cover your face with some kind of protection, and do not dust on a windy day.

An aerosol spray or dust bomb is handy to use for small invasions of insects. Aphids, for example, sometimes cluster on one or two bushes ignoring the rest. Using a bomb avoids dragging out your large equipment. But beware, some bombs are not designed to use on rose leaves.

*Try some simple methods of eliminating insect pests.*
1.   Early each spring, saturate all shade and flowering trees adjacent to the rose garden with a fungicidal spray.
2.   Aphids have been practically eliminated from my rose garden by the removal of one flowering crabapple tree.
3.   Fading blooms attract various types of bugs and an assortment of flying insects. By removing the flower before it is full-blown, you can discourage many of these pests from visiting the rose garden.
4.   Water-rinsing the foliage will wash away various worms, spidermites, and aphids. Rinse the plants early in the morning the day before you plan to spray.

*An old theory on pest control* is to plant marigolds, garlic, verbena, etc., in or near the rose bed. You can try any plan that pleases you, but marigold blooms attract Japanese beetles, and the worst invasion of spidermites I ever saw was in my beautiful pink rose garden on Cape Cod, where I had used pink Mayflower verbena as a ground cover.

## SYSTEMIC INSECTICIDES — ( NOT FUNGICIDES )

This is the new approach to controlling and killing insect pests. Systemic insecticides are applied as dry granules in solution or in pellet form to the surface soil and then watered in. One to four days later the chemicals are released to roots and then carried through the sap stream to new shoots, leaves, and flowers, supposedly giving protection from sucking insects for six weeks.

The original idea behind the development of systemics was to apply the chemicals to the roots to protect the foliage of plants from the constant insult of chemical application or dusting. This insect protection is supposed to last 6 weeks. It is still questionable whether the protection lasts longer than 10 to 12 days.

A systemic insecticide has now been developed to apply to the leaves. In my opinion, this is an absolute contradiction of the original purpose of systemic insecticides, for once again the foliage is subjected to chemical controls. Systemics contain chemicals that are harmful to human beings. These products in the hands of amateur gardeners are dangerous, for they may be inadvertently applied to roses planted near such things as parsley, lettuce, mint, and the usual herbs found in home gardens.

Another systemic combined with an inorganic food formula has appeared on the market. I do not approve of or recommend its use. Systemics should be used for the control of insect pests only. When combined with inorganic foods, there is a danger of overfeeding one or more unneeded inorganic elements and unbalancing the nutrient content of the soil.

Caution:

Before buying a systemic, read the label carefully. Follow the directions on the label exactly or you may seriously injure your plants or harm yourself if it contains chemicals that are dangerous for use on edible foods.

If leaves curl a few days after using a systemic, it may indicate an overdose of chemicals. Rinse the foliage thoroughly and saturate the soil. Systemics should be used with great care. They are still in the experimental stage.

## FUNGICIDES

A new fungicide effective against diseases of flowers and ornamentals is the new compound Benlate benomyl fungicide, now regarded by many agricultural researchers as a major breakthrough in plant disease control. On roses Benlate has been approved for the control of Blackspot, Powdery Mildew and Botrytis Gray Mold.

As a foliar spray Benlate has the unique property of penetrating plant tissue, providing local systemic protection within the leaf. Tests show Benlate has strong curative as well as favorable residual protective action.

Benlate is a wettable powder to be mixed with water for application as a spray. Application should begin when the disease first appears. Repeated applications on a ten to fourteen day schedule should be maintained throughout the growing season, or as long as needed. (Benlate may be used safely as often as every seven days as a preventive.)

Phaltan is still recommended when Blackspot first appears. Use in combination with Benlate.

Use: 2 teaspoons Phaltan, plus
 1 tablespoon Benlate to 2 gallons of water.

After two sprayings use the Benlate alone as often as every seven days to control further spread of Blackspot or Mildew.


ॐ DORMANT SPRAYS — (*fungicides*)


The use of dormant sprays, such as lime-sulphur or Bordeaux mixture, is recommended by some rosarians for control of fungus spores or insect eggs that may have overwintered on canes or in the ground. Some scientists are doubtful that these dormant sprays are as effective as claimed.

Dormant sprays have to be applied to canes early in spring before leaf buds show, or these strong chemicals will kill the new young shoots. They must never be applied when the temperature is expected to be 40° or below. Dormant sprays stain walls and painted surfaces.

Instead of trying to use dormant sprays wait until the young foliage is fairly well developed, then use Phaltan (fungicide). Saturate the canes, young foliage, and the surface soil. You will get excellent results and will not risk burning the tender new shoots. The

Phaltan treatment can be repeated in a week or ten days if it is deemed necessary.

All through this chapter I have listed specific insecticides and fungicides to use for an immediate problem, and have given the trade names of some combined controls. The longer you grow roses, the more you will realize this is not a good thing for an author to do, for scientists are improving rose controls so rapidly that what is written today may be obsolete tomorrow. If you are in doubt about a specific element or commercial product, ask your County or State Agricultural Agent for direction.

## EQUIPMENT NEEDED

A Hayes glass jar with a pressure spray to attach to hose, or any pressure sprayer that suits your needs. I prefer the Hayes jar because it has a long nozzle. There are others available.

> Duster — There are many types.
> Measuring spoons
> Large graduated measuring cup
> Bucket — 2½ gallon capacity
> Pad and pencil to work out formulas
> Hose — 50 feet or more

There is an excellent ten-gallon, gasoline driven power sprayer (2½ horse power) with a long nozzle and hose that is pushable and pull-able!

*Measurement Guide*

Measurements in cups and spoons mean level measuring cup and level measuring spoon.

*Teaspoons*

> 3 teaspoons = 1 tablespoon

*Tablespoons*

> 2 tablespoons = ⅛ cup or 1 fluid ounce

4 tablespoons = ¼ cup or 2 fluid ounces
8 tablespoons = ½ cup or ¼ pint
16 tablespoons = 1 cup or ½ pint

*Cupsful, pints, quarts*
2 cups = 1 pint or 16 fluid ounces
2 pints = 1 quart
4 quarts = 1 gallon

*Dry Weight*
1 ounce = approximately 2 tablespoonsful dry weight.

## CHEMICAL CONTROLS
### *Insecticides, Fungicides, Miticides*

*Acti-dione PM* — specific for powdery mildew. Use at 10 to 14 day intervals. More frequent spraying may cause injury to rose plants. Apply early in the day.
Mix:   2 level tablespoons to 1 gallon of water.

*Aramite* — miticide. Effective for red spidermites. Do not use on vegetables.
Mix: 1 tablespoon (15% wettable powder) to 1 gallon of water.

*Black Leaf 40* — nicotine sulphate. An old and one of the best controls of aphids, white flies, budworms, and leaf hoppers.
Mix: 1½ teaspoons to 1 gallon of water, plus 1 teaspoon soap powder or flakes as a spreader (not a detergent).
Use with care in hot weather — reduce the formula.

*Captan* — fungicide. Controls blackspot. Not effective for powdery mildew. Compatible with most insecticides. Do not combine with oil sprays or lime sulphur.
Mix:   3 level tablespoons to 1 gallon of water.

*Chlordane* — a contact insecticide used as soil treatment to kill Japanese beetle grubs, earwigs, ants. Available as emulsion, wettable powder, or dust.

*D.D.T.* — is used for the control of borers, Japanese beetles, cater-pillars, leaf hoppers, rose midge, rose slugs. D.D.T. is included in many commercial rose pesticides.
Mix: 1 tablespoon (50% wettable powder) to 1 gallon of water. Methoxoclor can be substituted for D.D.T. with excellent results.

*Fermate* (Ferbam) — fungicide. Effective for blackspot, maybe rust, not for powdery mildew. Included in some commercial rose dusts and sprays. Fermate leaves a dark disfiguring residue on flowers and leaves.

*Karathane* — an efficient fungicide for control of powdery mildew. Difficult to obtain.
Mix ½ teaspoon to 1 gallon of water.

*Kelthane* — miticide. Safe to handle. Excellent control.
Mix: 2 teaspoons to 1 gallon of water.

*Lime Sulphur* — dormant spray. For control of overwintering fungus spores and eggs. Must be applied while plants are dormant before leaf buds break.
Mix: 1 part lime sulphur to 9 parts of water.

*Lindane* — insecticide for control of aphids, thrips, and some beetles.
Mix: 1 tablespoon (25% wettable powder) to 1 gallon of water.

*Malathion* — insecticide. One of the best controls for aphids and white flies. Safe to use.
Mix: 1½ teaspoons (50% emulsion or 50% wettable powder) to 1 gallon of water

*Methoxoclor* — replaces D.D.T. in some rose sprays and dusts. A safe substitute for D.D.T.
Mix. 2 teaspoons (15% wettable powder) to 1 gallon of water.

*Phaltan* (Folpet) — fungicide. Probably the best control for black-spot.
Mix: 1 tablespoon to 1 gallon of water.

*Sevin* (Carbaryl) — effective for control of Japanese beetles, some caterpillars, and sawflies. Toxic to bees and many beneficial insects.
Mix: 2 tablespoons (50% wettable powder) to 1 gallon of water.

# Winter Protection

*Winter cover* is used in cold regions of the country to protect rose plants from wintry blasts and rapid changes of temperature. It is a controversial subject, many rosarians now believing protection to be needed only where temperatures approach or dip below 10° above zero. Continuous freezing temperatures, when roses are covered under a blanket of snow, are not as serious as when the temperature alternates between freezing and thawing. No cover is needed in milder climates.

The type of cover and how much of it to use has to be determined by the severity of winter weather in your locality.

*Winter protection* actually begins in early spring and continues throughout the growing season, for plants that have been well fed and kept disease-free during the summer go into their dormant winter period with a better chance of surviving than do plants defoliated by disease, insect pests, or neglect.

## WINTERIZE YOUR PLANTS

*Hardening* the rose plants in late summer helps them to survive the rigors of winter.

1. After August fifteenth change the feeding program. Stop using nitrogenous root foods; this will discourage the development of new, succulent growth.

2. Foliar food may be applied up to September 15 if needed, for nitrogen fed in this form is rapidly used and does not encourage the development of too much new growth.

3. Early in September minimize watering, but be sure to keep the ground moist until it freezes.

4. Stop all pruning. Remove only diseased or dead wood.

5. Cut flowers with short stems only.

6. Remember, saving every inch of wood means *winter food for the rose*, because canes store carbohydrates for use by the rose during the dormant period.

Don't panic! An early freeze in October is beneficial to the rose. This is Nature's way of slowing the growing rhythm.

If you lose a few plants from winter-kill, don't blame yourself too much. Some rose varieties are hardier than others.

### Soil Mounding Method

There are many ways to winterize roses, but the mounding method described below I believe to be the easist and best for use in moderate to cold regions, if you get someone to haul dirt to the rose garden!

1. Before the first hard freeze, remove as many dead leaves as possible from plants and rose bed. Carefully clean the beds of all debris and burn the trash.

2. Water the earth well before making the soil mounds. Roses can

be seriously injured if their roots are dry when the ground freezes.
3.  If some plants have developed very tall canes, do not prune back.
Cut off a few inches of the tips and tie the canes firmly together to
prevent them from being whipped about by winter winds.
4.  Now bring enough soil to the rose bed to make hillocks, ten or
more inches high, *around the crown and up into the branches of the
bushes*. Pack the soil to prevent washing and to hold the plants
secure during winter storms.

*Mounding and Wire Collar Methods*

Caution:
*Never dig soil from around the bush* to make the mounds — digging
disturbs the plant's superficial roots.
*Never use manure or leaves* to make the mounds.  These materials

cause cane rot by keeping the plants too moist during the winter months.

5. Cover the valleys between hillocks with more soil, manure, or leaves four to six inches deep. This extra cover between the mounds gives better root protection and decreases the chance of soil erosion during heavy winter rains.

6. Keep the soil moist until the ground freezes.

7. An extra cover of fir or pine boughs lightly laid over the bed after the earth is hard protects the canes from winter sun and wind and is a good protection in any region.

Caution:

Be careful not to make this extra cover too compact; you may invite mice to make this their winter home. These varmints gnaw the canes and cause more damage than the wintry weather.

*Salt hay* encourages diseases and is difficult to remove in spring.

### *Wire Collar Method*

Collars made of various materials are used to bed down the rose plant, but wire collars seem to be the most popular.

Cut half-inch mesh hardware cloth into 10 or 12 inch strips, 3 to 4 feet long. Make a collar by hooking the ends together. Place collar around plant and fill with light soil. Tying canes together facilitates putting wire collars into place. Wire collars can be stored and used for many years.

### *Seaweed: use as winter mulch*

Dried seaweed makes an excellent organic winter mulch and is readily available for seashore gardens. Make earth hillocks, then spread dry seaweed for added protection.

### *Climbers*

Climbers are hardy plants and most of them survive without winter protection. However, in extremely cold climates, remove canes from their supports while the canes are still pliant, lay them on the ground, hold them in place with crossed stakes and cover with evergreen branches (not leaves). Mound earth around the crown of the plant. Be sure the earth has been well watered before the ground freezes.

*Standard or Tree Roses*

To winterize tree roses, find a good spot in the garden where you can dig a trench or pit a foot deep and large enough to accommodate all your tree roses when placed side by side. Save all the dirt removed from the trench to use for covering the plants.

1. Cut back all canes to approximately 14 inches from the center of the bush. If canes are pliable, tie them together.

2. Dig your plants carefully after the first frost in the fall.

3. Lay the trees side by side in the trench and lightly cover the entire plant with soil.

4. Then, for protection from field mice and moles, lay a cover of hardware cloth over the entire area.

5. Continue replacing soil until the earth is well above ground level.

6. For added winter protection, cover the area with branches and leaves.

If burying your rose trees is too difficult to accomplish, protection can also be given by wrapping the entire trunk and head with layers of hay wrapped with sacking, and a plastic or vinyl cover tied around it. Next, place some hay over the head and cover with sacking to

protect the head from the sun. Lay a square of plastic over the sacking and tie down the four corners to the trunk. This allows for air and precludes any chance of water getting into the wrappings around the trunk to cause rot. Be sure to mound the earth high around the cane.

Do not open the wrappings too early in the spring. Remove a little at a time from the trunk. Leave the hat until last.

### Miniature Roses

Miniature roses are hardy. In extremely cold regions, before the ground freezes, mound soil 3 to 4 inches in and around the plants. Moisten the soil and lightly cover with fir boughs. No winter protection is needed in warm climates.

### Pillar Roses

Roses tied to posts or columns must be protected from winter sun, whipping winds, and rapid changes of temperature. Protect them by mounding the earth up and around the base, and then lay evergreen boughs over the canes. Remove cover in early spring a little at a time. Be sure to keep the boughs handy in case of an unexpected freeze.

# It's Spring Again

## ℰ THERE'S WORK TO DO

You may not know it's spring when a light dusting of snow covers the ground in mid-March, but your roses know and they want attention. Actually, this is the busiest time of the year for the rosarian-gardener, for there are many jobs to be done to ready the beds and the roses for the coming blooming season. In warmer climates your rose garden chores begin weeks earlier.

If possible, enlist the help of an enthusiastic assistant. You'll get the chores done more quickly and better than if you tackle the job alone.

ॐ◆SPRING CHORES

Working time and duplication of effort can be saved if you carry out the following instructions in the order given.

*Tools Needed*

Trowel
Sharp pruning shears
Lopping shears
Narrow iron-toothed rake
Bamboo rake
Pointed shovel
Wheelbarrow
Canvas or burlap bags for easy removal of earth taken from beds.
Sprayer or duster (preferably sprayer)
Fertilizers needed (*See Feeding, p. 72*)
Bucket
Watering can
Measuring spoon for chemicals

*Begin Your Chores*

1.  Remove any protective boughs or leaves and half the earth mound.
2.  Several days later, when the plants have recovered from the shock of exposure to the elements, remove the remaining part of the earth mound. The earth used for mounds should be discarded and used elsewhere in the garden, for if this extra earth were cultivated into the soil year after year, the bed would be too high to apply a mulch without smothering the bud union.
3.  Using a trowel, take *soil samples* from several places in the rose bed, mix samples, dry naturally, and send to your State Agricultural

Agent for analysis. Enclose a note stating that the tests are needed for rose culture.

4. Prune any obviously dead canes or dead tops (dieback) to facilitate cleaning the beds.

5. Rake and level the beds. (Burn debris.)

6. Saturate canes and surface soil with a *fungicide spray.*

7. As an extra precaution have all trees and shrubs adjacent to the rose garden sprayed with a dormant spray. This early protective spray may kill dormant insects and their eggs as well as overwintering fungi.

8. Next, give the roses their first meal of the year. (*See Feeding, p. 79*)

9. Prune your roses. (*See Pruning, p. 83*)

10. Rake beds clean of all debris and apply two or three inches of organic foods and humus. Cultivate this layer carefully into top soil and water thoroughly.

11. Then, some lovely spring day when young shoots are well developed, once again clean and level the bed, soak the soil, and apply the mulch. (*See Mulches, p. 61*)

Now is the time to stand back, admire your handiwork, and wait for the thrill of seeing the first rose buds burst into bloom.

# GLOSSARY

ACID SOIL —— *a low pH rating meaning acid, not alkaline.*

ALKALINE SOIL —— *a high pH rating caused by native alkaline soil or overliming*

ATTAR —— *the pure oil extracted of roses.*

BASAL BREAK —— *A new and valuable cane that starts from the bud union.*

BREAK —— *the start of a new stem, leaf stem, or cane from a bud eye.*

BUD —— *an immature flower. "Bud" is also used to describe that part of a rose cane used to graft onto a different variety of rose.*

BUD EYE —— *the small, swollen node on a cane, the beginning of a new leaf stem or flower stem.*

BUD UNION —— *the enlarged node at the top of shank above the roots created by budding a rose variety onto the cane of a sturdy, fast-growing understock.*

CANE —— *the main stalk of a rose plant that bears leaves, flowers, and seed pods (hips).*

CHELATES —— *chemicals that aid in releasing iron and other minor elements in the soil. Used to cure chlorosis.*

CHLOROPHYLL —— *green coloring matter important to the development of healthy green leaves.*

CHLOROSIS —— *loss of leaf chlorophyll (green coloring matter).*

DEFOLIATE —— *loss of foliage due to diseased leaves, chemical injury, or insect invasions, etc.*

DISBUDDING —— *the removal of immature buds.*

EMULSION —— *a heavy water-soluble oil.*

EYE — *the bud eye or beginning of a leaf stem on a cane.*

FEEDER ROOTS —— *hair or fibrous secondary roots.*

FOLIAR FOODS —— *a chemical combination of inorganic elements, vitamins, and hormones, fed by application to the rose leaves.*

FRIABLE —— *porous, open-textured soil that permits water and oxygen to permeate and reach deep roots.*

FUNGICIDES —— *chemicals used to control or destroy fungus infection of plants.*

GRAFTING —— *a means of propagating new rose varieties.*

GROUND LIMESTONE —— *a natural product used to correct acid soil.*

HARDY —— *indicates ability of plants to survive cold and other unfavorable weather conditions.*

HEAVY SOIL —— *non-porous or non-friable clay soil.*

HILLOCK —— *the mound made by placing soil around the base of a plant for winter protection.*

HIP —— *seed pod or rose fruit.*

HUMUS —— *decaying organic matter such as compost, leaf mold, etc.*

HYBRIDIZE —— *a special method of crossing two different species or varieties of roses.*

INORGANIC FERTILIZERS —— *major chemical or mineral elements.*

INSECTICIDES —— *chemicals designed to kill or control insect pests.*

LIMESTONE (LIME) —— *an important natural mineral used to correct acid soil conditions.*

LARVAE — *immature insect pests.*

LOAM —— *a natural soil mixture of clay, soil, and humus.*

LOCKS —— *a term used to express the condition which renders nutrients unavailable in the soil, caused by over-liming or highly alkaline soil.*

MICROCLIMATE —— *air circulation.*

MITICIDES —— *chemicals used to kill or control mites such as red spidermites.*

MOUNDING —— *placing soil around the base of a plant and up into the canes for winter protection.*

NATIVE SOIL —— *natural soil.*

NITROGENOUS —— *referring to the inorganic element, nitrogen.*

NUTRIENT —— *a nutritive substance or ingredient.*

ORGANIC FOOD —— *derived from decaying organisms and plant life.*

ORGANIC MATTER —— *source of organic food.*

pH —— *referring to acid or alkaline soil condition.*

SHANK —— *the area between the big roots and the bud union.*

SOIL —— *top layer of earth that can be tilled.*

SOUR SOIL —— *acid pH rating.*

SPECIES ROSA —— *ancient parent stock.*

SPONGY —— *capable of holding moisture, such as peat moss.*

SPORT —— *a single cane that develops spontaneously showing distinct characteristics that differ from those of the parent plant.*

STEM —— *a small cane that develops leaves or ends in a flower bud.*

STOCK —— *parent variety of rose.*

SUCKER —— *an unwanted cane of the understock variety that starts below the bud union.*

SWEET SOIL —— *alkaline pH rating.*

WETTABLE POWDER —— *a fungicide or insecticide that can be dissolved in water for application to the rose plant.*

# VISIT PUBLIC ROSE GARDENS AND NURSERIES

In every state and in most large cities there are rose gardens far too numerous to list. When visiting a city in June or July, inquire from the Chamber of Commerce or in advance, ask the American Rose Society for a list of public and private gardens that are open to visitors.

Almost all accredited nurseries are open to the public. Since these are the sources from which we buy our roses, it is an exciting adventure for the beginner or amateur rosarian to see the great fields of roses when in bloom and to discuss the potentials of the various varieties with the grower. You will always receive a courteous welcome and can order your roses while visiting the nursery.

## SOME ROSE GARDENS IN THE UNITED STATES

*Elizabeth Park, Municipal Rose Garden, Hartford, Connecticut*
One of Connecticut's beautiful municipal rose gardens.

*Hershey Rose Garden, Hershey, Pennsylvania*
On 23 acres, there are 42,000 rose bushes and 1,200 varieties. The blooming season is from June 1 to June 30. Admission and parking free.

*Jackson and Perkins Rose Gardens, Newark, New York*
This 17-acre rose garden contains more than 36,000 rose plants. Every important variety may be seen in formal, mass plantings, or in informal type gardens. These gardens are open from June until the first killing frost in Autumn. Admission free.

*Will Tillotson's Roses, Brown's Valley Road, Watsonville, Calif.*
You can not only visit this garden at certain times of year, but this is the finest source from which to buy old, rare, and historic roses.

*Exposition Park Rose Garden, Los Angeles, California*
16,000 roses.

*Municipal Rose Garden, Oakland, California*
8,000 roses.

*Rose Hills Memorial Park, Whittier, California*
4,000 roses.

*Shoreham Hotel Rose Garden, Washington, D.C.*
1,200 roses.

*Municipal Rose Garden, Caldwell, Idaho*
5,500 roses.

*Marquette Park Rose Garden, Chicago, Illinois*
5,000 roses.

*Robert R. McCormick Memorial Gardens, Wheaton, Illinois*
1,000 roses.

*Lakeside Rose Garden, Fort Wayne, Indiana*
5,000 roses.

*Municipal Rose Garden, Davenport, Iowa*
2,800 roses.

*Reinisch Rose Gardens, Topeka, Kansas*
9,000 roses.

*Municipal Rose Garden, Minneapolis, Minnesota*
5,000 roses.

*Missouri Botanical Garden, St. Louis, Missouri*
5,000 roses.

*Cranford Rose Garden, Brooklyn, New York*
4,000 roses.

*New York Botanical Garden, Bronx, New York*
7,000 roses.

*Maplewood Park Rose Garden, Rochester, New York*
7,200 roses.

*Sterling Forest Gardens, Tuxedo, New York*
4,000 roses.

*Park of Roses, Columbus, Ohio*
35,000 roses.

*International Rose Garden, Portland, Oregon*
10,000 roses.

*Dallas Garden Center AARS Garden, Dallas, Texas*
15,000 roses.

*Tyler Rose Park, Tyler, Texas*
38,000 roses.

*Municipal Rose Garden, Salt Lake City, Utah*
9,000 roses.

*Woodland Park Rose Garden, Seattle, Washington*
5,100 roses.

*Rose Hill, Manito Park, Spokane, Washington*
5,800 roses.

*Whitnall Park, Boerner Botanical Gardens, Hales Corners, Wisconsin*
5,000 roses.


## FAMOUS ROSE GARDENS OF EUROPE


*Golden Walk, Chartwell, England*
The Golden Walk at Chartwell, England, the home of Sir Winston and Lady
Churchill, was planted in 1958, as a gift from their family to celebrate their
golden wedding. There are 50 standards (tree roses) in 28 different varieties
and about 300 bushes along this golden walk.

*Parc de Bagatelle, Bois de Boulogne, Paris, France*
Do not fail to visit the Parc de Bagatelle during the rose season. It is one
of the most exquisite gardens in the world. The Rose Show is from June 1
to June 30, but the park is open daily from May 1 to September 15.

*Parc de la Grange, Geneva, Switzerland*
This decorative garden overlooks Lac Leman. It is embellished with fountains and beautiful statuary and is maintained by the city of Geneva.

*Parque del Oeste, Madrid, Spain*
This is one of the most beautiful rose gardens in the world, and should be
visited by all travelers who love roses.

*Queen Mary Rose Garden, Regent's Park, London, England*
When in London, do not overlook this beautiful garden.

*Roseraie de l'Hay-Les-Roses, Sceaux, Paris, France*
Here can be seen all of the varieties grown in the garden for the pleasure of
the Empress Josephine in the early 1800's at the Chateau de Malmaison.
This garden of 25,000 rose plants is in fact a museum of roses. It is only
7 miles south of Paris and is open from 10:00 a.m. to 6:00 p.m. daily
from the last Sunday in May or the first Sunday in June to July 10.

There are many beautiful rose gardens not listed here. Be sure to inquire of
your travel bureau while making your itinerary or you may miss a beautiful
rose display.

# BIBLIOGRAPHY

Allen, Harold H., *Roses — Growing for Exhibiting*, Princeton, New Jersey, D. Van Nostrand Company, Inc., 1961

Allen, R. C., *Roses for Every Garden*, New York, M. Barrows and Co., Inc., 1962

Bois, Eric, and Trechslin, Anne-Marie, *Roses*, Zurich, Thomas Nelson and Sons, Ltd.

Brooklyn Botanical Garden, *A Handbook on Roses*, Brooklyn, 1965

Bush-Brown, James and Louise, *America's Garden Book*, New York and London, Charles Scribner's Sons, 1958

Coats, Peter, *Roses*, New York, G. P. Putnam's Sons

Edwards, Gordon, *Roses For Enjoyment*, London, W. H. & L. Collingridge Ltd., 1962

Edwards, John Paul, *How To Grow Roses*, Menlo Park, California, Lane Book Company, 1963

Encyclopedia Americana

Encyclopedia Brittanica

Fairbrother, F., *Roses*, Norwich, England, Jarrod & Sons, Ltd., 1963 — prepared in collaboration with the Royal Horticultural Society.

Genders, Roy, *Miniature Roses*, London, England, Blandford Press, 1960

Gordon, Jean, *Pageant of the Rose*, Woodstock, Vermont, Red Rose Publications, 1961

Kordes, William, *Roses*, New York, Reinhold Publishing Company, 1964.

Lester, Francis E., *My Friend the Rose*, Harrisburg, Pa., Mount Pleasant Press, J. Horace McFarland Co.

Lewis, C. H. and Allen, R. C. (editors), *What Every Rose Grower Should Know*, American Rose Society, 1966

Mannering, Eva, *The Best of Redoute's Roses*, New York, The Viking Press

McFarland, J. Horace, and Pyle, Robert, *How To Grow Roses*, New York, MacMillan Company, 1949

Milton, John, *Rose Growing Simplified*, New York, Hearthside Press, Inc., 1962

Moore, Ralph S., *All About Miniature Roses*, Kansas City, Mo., Diversity Press, 1966

Norman, A., *Successful Rose Growing*, London, W. H. & L. Collingridge Ltd., 1962

Park, Bertram, *The Guide To Roses*, Princeton, New Jersey, D. Van Nostrand Company, Inc., 1956

Park, Bertram, *Roses — The Cultivation of the Rose*, Royal National Rose Society, London and Tanbridge, Whitefriars Press, Ltd., 1963

Park, Bertram, *The World of Roses*, New York, E. P. Dutton & Company

Pinney, Margaret E., *The Miniature Rose Book*, Princeton, New Jersey, D. Van Nostrand Co., Inc., 1964

Rockwell, E. F., and Grayson, Esther G., *Complete Book of Roses*, Garden City, New York, Doubleday and Company, Inc., 1958

Stemler, Dorothy, *The Book of Old Roses*, Boston, Mass., Bruce Humphries, 1966

Thomas, Graham Stuart, *Climbing Roses Old and New*, New York, St. Martin's Press, 1965.

Thomas, Graham Stuart, *Shrub Roses of Today*, London, Phoenix House, Ltd., 1964

Thompson, M. M. "Doc", *Rose Pruning With Pictures*, Los Angeles, California, Mary Lynn and Asso., 1960

Thomson, Richard, *Old Roses for Modern Gardens*, Princeton, New Jersey, D. Van Nostrand Co., Inc., 1959

Thomson, Richard, and Wilson, Helen Van Pelt, *Roses For Pleasure*, Princeton, New Jersey, D. Van Nostrand Company, Inc., 1957

Tillotson's Roses, *Roses of Yesterday and Today*, Watsonville, California, 1964 (catalog)

Webster's New World Dictionary of the American Language — College Edition, Cleveland and New York, World Publishing Company, 1959

Webster's Seventh New Collegiate Dictionary, Springfield, Massachusetts, G. & C. Merriam Company, 1965

Westcott, Cynthia, *Anyone Can Grow Roses*, Princeton, New Jersey, D. Van Nostrand Company, Inc., all editions

Westcott, Cynthia, *The Gardener's Bug Book*, Garden City, New York, Doubleday & Co., Inc., 1964

Wilson, Helen Van Pelt, *Climbing Roses*, New York, M. Barrows and Company, Inc., 1955


*The Rose*, London

Dick, A., "Growing Modern Roses in Scotland — II, Pruning and Feeding," Spring 1964

Wallace, B. S. T., "Know Your Rose Roots," Winter 1964-65

Whitehead, Stanley B., "pH and Roses," Spring 1964

*The Rose Annual,* The Royal National Rose Society, St. Albans, England, 1965-1966

Coggiatti, Stelvio, "Roses & Rome, Yesterday and Today," 1965

Borchard, Ruth, "Of Very Ancient Roses," 1966

Graham, Thomas, "On Starting a Collection of Shrub Roses," 1966

West, Graham, "The Role of Magnesium in Rose Culture," 1966


*American Rose Annual,* American Rose Society, Columbus, Ohio

Barke, Harvey E., "Pest Control in Roses," 1965

Beach, O. R., "Fertilizers and Disease/Insect Problems," 1966

Bowles, Orville, E., "Our Chemical Fertilizers," 1965

Dasher, Ralph M., "Keep It Simple!" 1965

Hanan, Joe J., "Roses and Soil," 1964

Howland, Dr. Joseph E., "Is Your Microclimate Killing Your Roses?" 1964

Irvine, Kenneth C., "Roses in New England," 1962

Jacklin, S. W. and Smith, Floyd F., "Excluding Flower Thrips from Outdoor Roses," 1964

Jorgenson, Dr. George & Nora, "Foliar Feeding Ten Years Later," 1962

Lucks, Hartl, "Let's Look Inside," 1964

Miller, Dr. P. W., "A Down to Earth Approach to Rose Growing," 1962

Morey, Dennison, "The Compensation Point," 1964

Stewart, Robert N., and Semeniuk, Peter, "Report on Rose Research in the U. S. Dept. of Agriculture," 1965

Traylor, Jack A., Wagnon, H. Keith, and Williams, Harold, "Should We Be Concerned With Virus Diseases in Roses?" 1964

Tukey, H. B., Jr., "Leaching of Nutrients from Plant Foliage by Rain and Mist," 1964

Went, F. W., "The Importance of the Root System for the Growing of Roses," 1964

# ACCREDITED ROSE GROWERS OF THE
# UNITED STATES AND CANADA

ARP Roses, Inc.
P.O. Box 3338
Tyler, Texas 75705

Armstrong Nurseries
P.O. Box 473
Ontario, Calif. 91764

Breedlove Nursery
P.O. Box 450
Tyler, Texas 75705

Brightridge Rose Co.
(Brownell Sub-Zero Roses)
125 Brightridge Avenue
East Providence, Rhode Island

Carroll Gardens
Box 310
Westminster, Md. 21157

Conard-Pyle Co. (Star Roses)
West Grove, Pa. 19390

Crombie Rose Nurseries
34595 Alvarado Niles Rd.
Union City, Calif. 94587

Eddie's Nurseries
4100 S. W. Marine Dr.
Vancouver 13, B.C., Canada

Ellesmere Nurseries
R.R. No. 1
Brooklin, Ontario, Canada

Elmer Roses
4273 Riverside Drive
Chino, California 91710

Emlong Nurseries, Inc.
Stevensville, Mich. 49127

Evergreens, Inc.
275 N. Hubbards Lane
Louisville, Kentucky 40207

Roy Hennessey's (Old Roses)
Scappoose, Oregon 97056

Paul J. Howard's California Flowerland
11700 National Blvd.
Los Angeles 64, California

Ilgenfritz Nurseries, Inc.
Telegraph & Dunbar Rds.
Monroe, Mich 48161

Inter-State Nursery
Hamburg, Iowa 51640

Jackson & Perkins Co.
P.O. Box 266, Newark, New York, *also*
204 Rose Lane, Pleasanton, Calif. 94566

Kelly Bros. Nursery
23 Maple Street
Dansville, New York 14437

Joseph J. Kern Nursery
Box 33, Mentor, Ohio 44060

E. V. Kimbrew
Wills Point, Texas 75169

Krider Nurseries, Inc.
Middlebury, Indiana 46540

McConnell Nursery Co.
Port Burwell, Ontario, Canada

Mini-Roses
Box 4255
Dallas, Texas 75208

Modern Rose Nursery
R.R. 2, Altona Rd., Pickering
Ontario, Canada

Roselawn Nurseries
P.O. Drawer 438
Winnsboro, Texas 75494

Roses by Edmunds
P.O. Box 68
Wilsonville, Oregon 97070

Roseway Nurseries
2935 S.W. 234th Avenue
Rt. 2, Beaverton, Oregon 97005

Sequoia Nursery (miniatures)
2915 E. Mineral King
Visalia, California 93277

R. H. Shumway
628 Cedar Street
Rockford, Illinois 61101

Stanek's Garden Center
East 2929 27th Avenue
Spokane, Washington 99233

Stark Brothers
Louisiana, Missouri 63353

Stern's Nurseries
Geneva, New York 14456

Stocking Rose Nursery
12525 N. Capitol Avenue
San Jose, California 95133

P.O. Tate Nursery
Rt. 3, Box 307
Tyler, Texas 75705

Thomasville Nurseries, Inc. (tea roses)
P.O. Box 7
Thomasville, Georgia 31792

Will Tillotson
802 Brown Valley Road
Watsonville, California 95076

Ty-Tex
P.O. Box 532
Tyler, Texas 75702

N. Van Hevelingen
P.O. Box 5076
Portland, Oregon 97213

Wayside Gardens Co.
Mentor, Ohio 44060

Percy H. Wright
6407 109th Street
Saskatoon, Saskatchewan, Canada

Melvin E. Wyant
Rose Specialist, Inc.
Johnny Cake Ridge

Wyatt & Quarles Seed Co. (Star Roses)
327 S. Wilmington Street
Raleigh, North Carolina 27601
Mentor, Ohio 44060

# INDEX

Accredited rose growers, 151, 152
Acid soil, 44
  correcting acid conditions, 45
  glossary, 142
  pH, 44, 45, 46
  test your soil, 43
Acti-Dione PM, 99, 129
Air circulation (micro-climate),
  36
Alkaline soil, 45
  glossary, 142
  lower alkalinity, 45
  pH, 44
  slightly alkaline, 45
  test your soil, 43
American Rose Society, 20
Aphid, 116, 127
  illustration, 116
Aramite (miticide), 120, 128
Attar of roses, 12, 15
  glossary, 142

Basal break
  glossary, 142
Basal canes, 90, 87
Bibliography, 148-150
Black Leaf 40 (nicotine sul-
  phate), 116, 120, 129
Black Spot, 96, 97, 98
  illustration, 96
Blood Meal, 75, 76, 79
Bone Meal, 75, 76, 79
Bordeaux Mixture (dormant
  spray), 102
Borers, 103, 117
Buckwheat hulls, 62
Buds
  glossary, 142
Bud eye, 86, 87
  glossary, 142
Bud union, 54, 84, 85, 86
  glossary, 142
Burying roses, 52, 136
Buying rose plants,
  where and how, 16, 17

Cabbage rose, 29
  see R. centifolia, 31
Calcium, 74
  deficiency, 106, 199
Candelabra canes, 90
Cane, 85, 86, 89
  glossary, 142
Canker
  cane canker, 101
  crown canker, 105
  wound fungi, 101, 102
Captan, 99, 130
Carpenter Bee, 117
Catalogs, 17
Caterpillars (leaf-roller), 119
Chelates,
  glossary, 142
Cherokee rose,
  legend of, 14
  R. laevigata, 34
China tea roses, 32
  R. chinensis, 32
  R. gigantea, 32
  R. odorata ochralenca, 33
Chlordane, 118, 130
Chlorophyll, 105
Chlorosis, 81, 105
  common causes, 106, 112
Clay soil, 40, 41
Climbers, 25, 27
Cocoa bean hulls, 62, 63
Compost, 42
Corn cobs, 61, 64
Cottonseed meal, 75, 76
Cow manure, 63, 75, 77
  composted, 77
  dehydrated, 77
Crown canker, 105
Crown gall, 104
  illustration, 104

D.D.T., 118, 120, 121, 130
Damask roses (R. damascena),
  15, 29, 30
  R. damascena bifera, 30

R. damascena trigintipetala, 30
Dieback, 86, 103, 104
  illustration, 103
Disbudding, 90
  glossary, 142
  illustration, 91
Diseases of roses, 94, 95
Dog rose,
  R. canina, 14
Dormant sprays, 127, 128

Epsom Salts, 82, 108
Eye, 86, 87
  glossary, 142

Fall planting, 18, 51
  delayed, 52
  protection, 57, 58
Feeder roots, 71
  glossary, 142
Feeding roses,
  balance the diet, 72
  established roses, 78-82
  newly planted roses, 82
Fermate, 130
Fertilizers,
  inorganic, 72, 73
  minor or trace elements, 74
  organic, 72, 75
Fish emulsion, 75, 76, 80
Fish Meal, 75, 76
Floribunda (hybrid jolyantha),
  21, 24
Foliar foods, 73, 79, 81
  glossary, 142
Friable soil, 40, 42
  glossary, 142
Fungicides, 130, 131
  glossary, 142
Fungus diseases, 95, 96
  black spot, 96
  mildew, 98
  rust, 100

Gallica roses,
  R. gallica officinalis, 30

R. rubra, 29
Gardens to visit
  Europe, 147
  United States, 145, 146
Grass clippings, 61, 64
Grass roots, 37
Ground leaves, 61, 62, 63
Ground tree bark, 61, 62, 63

Hips (rose fruit), 28
History, 11-15
Humus, 39, 41
  available sources, 42
  glossary, 143
Hybrid polyantha (floribunda),
  24
Hybrid tea roses, 22
  illustrations, 22, 23
  planting distance, 38
Hybridizing, 15, 16
  glossary, 143

Inorganic fertilizers (chemical-
  mineral), 115
  dry foods, 78
  foliar foods, 78
  liquid foods or emulsions, 78
Insect pests, 115-123
Insecticides, 130, 131
  glossary, 143
Iron, 74
  add iron to the diet, 81
  iron deficiency, 106, 107

Japanese Beetles, 118
  illustration, 118

Karathane, 130
Kelthane, 120, 130

Leaf Cutter Bee, 117
  illustration, 117
Leaf Hopper, 118
  illustration, 119
Leaf mold, 42

Leaf-roller (caterpillar), 119
Lime
    glossary, 143
    how to apply, 45
    limestone, 44, 45
    see pH, 44
Lindane, 120, 130
Liquid rose foods, 78, 80, 81
Loam, 39, 40
    glossary, 143

Magnesium
    deficiency, 106, 107, 108
    illustration, 108
Malathion, 116, 120, 130
Malnutrition,
    see Chlorosis, 105
Methoxychlor, 121, 131
Mildew, 9, 95, 98, 99, 100
    illustration, 98
Miniature roses, 27
    illustration, 26
Minor or trace elements, 74
Mites (red spider), 119
    illustration, 119
Modern garden roses, 21-27
    illustrations, 22, 23, 24, 25, 26
Mulches, 61, 62
    how to apply, 64
    when to apply, 65

Nitrogen, 73
    deficiency, 106, 109
    excess of, 73
    glossary, 143
    illustration, 109

Old, rare, and historic roses, 28-35
Organic fertilizers (nature's food) available sources, 75-77
Organic matter, 39, 41
    glossary, 143
Oxygen
    deficiency, 110, 111

illustration, 111

Pasture rose
    R. carolina, 33
Peat, 42
    see Mulches, 62, 63
    acidifying agent, 45
    soil conditioner, 48
Pests
    see Insect Pests, 115
pH, 44
    acid-alkaline soil, 44
    glossary, 143
    soil testing, 43
Phaltan (Folpet), 131
Phosphorus, 73, 74
    deficiency, 112
Phytotoxicity, 124
Pine needles,
    see Mulches, 62, 64
Pillar rose, 24, 27
    illustration, 25
Planting instructions, 52, 53, 54
    illustrations, 55, 56
    when to remove protection, 56, 57
Polyantha rose, 24, 25
Potash (potassium), 73, 74
    deficiency, 113
    illustration, 113
Potted and packaged roses
    buying, 19
    illustrations, 58, 59
    planting, 58, 59
Prairie rose
    R. setigera, 34
Preparing the rose bed, 47, 48, 49
Pruning, 83
    dieback, 86, 103
    fall, 93
    illustrations, 8, 85, 87, 88, 91, 92
    spring 83
    summer, 90

winter-kill, 86
Purple spotting, 114

Rambler rose, 28
Rapid-gro, 78
  foliar feed, 80
  root feed, 80, 81
Roots, 71
  planting instructions, 54
  root feeding, 78, 79, 80
Root thieves, 37
Rose Budworm, 120
Rose foods (dry, liquid foods,
  emulsions, foliar foods), 78
Royal National Rose Society, 21
Rust, 94, 95, 100
  illustrations, 100, 101

Sawdust, 62, 64
Seaweed, 62, 64
Sevin (Carbaryl), 131
Sheep manure, 75
  composted, 77
Shrubs roses, 27
Soil, 39, 40
  clay, 40, 41
  "fill", 41
  loam, 40, 41
  sand, 40, 41
  top soil, 40
Soil testing, 43
Sour soil
  glossary, 143
Species rosa, 33
  glossary, 144
  R. alba, 31
  R. banksiae, 33
  R. californica, 33
  R. canina (Dog Rose), 14, 33
  R. carolina (Pasture Rose), 33
  R. centifolia (Cabbage Rose),
    31
  R. chinensis, 32
  R. damascena, 15, 30
  R. damascena bifera, 30
  R. damascena trigintipetala, 30

R. eglanteria (Eglantine or
  Sweetbriar Rose), 33
R. gallica (R. rubra), 29
R. gallica officinalis, 30
R. gigantea, 33
R. hugonis (Golden Rose of
  China, 34
R. laevigata (Cherokee Rose),
  14, 34
R. moschata (Musk Rose), 31
R. multiflora (R. polyantha),
  25, 34
R. odorata ochroleuca, 33
R. rugosa, 34
R. setigera (Prairie Rose), 34
R. soulieana, 34
R. spinosissima, 35
R. spinosissima, altaica, 35
R. virgianna, 35
R. wichuriana, 35
"Sports"
  glossary, 144
  see climbers, 27
    moss roses, 34
Spraying and dusting, 94, 123
Spring chores, 139
Spring planting, 18
  delayed, 51
  illustration, 56
  protection, 56, 57
  roses arrive, 51
Stem,
  glossary, 144
Sucker cane, 86
  glossary, 144
  illustration, 85
Sunshine, 37
Sweet soil, 45
  glossary, 144
Sweetbriar rose,
  R. eglanteria, 33
Systemic insecticides, 126

Tedion, 120
Thrips, 123

illustration, 123
Trace elements, 74
Transpiration, 66
Transplanting, 59, 60
Tree roses, 27
   illustration, 26
   winter protection, 136

Understock, 16

Virus infection, 113, 114
   illustration, 114

Watering, 66, 67, 68
   how and when, 67
   illustration, 69

watering equipment, 68, 69, 70
Wettable powder,
   glossary, 144
Whale (liquid), 75, 77
   White Flies, 122
Winter cover for tree roses, 136
   illustration, 136
Winter protection, 132
   illustration, 134
   mulching, 135
   soil mounding method, 133, 134
Wire collars, 134
Winterize your plants, 133
   Winter-kill, 86